AUTHENTIC SEXY TRUTH

ONE WOMAN'S JOURNEY FROM NEW ORLEANS TO NEW MEXICO

TRACI ANN

AUTHENTIC
SEXY
TRUTH

First Print Edition

Dedication

*To all the lovely, magical people in my life
who inspired the writing of this book.*

Table of Contents

Dear Reader   9
Disclaimer   10

Part One: New Orleans   13

Dear Steph   15
Steely Intention   19
Baton Rouge Freedom Cry   21
Rainy with a Chance of Brass   27
Sunday Funday   31
Storage Unit   33
Story of Stuff, Home, and Betty   35

Part Two: Atlanta   37

10 to 65 to 85   39
Magic Bagels and Running Under Rainbows   43
Ode to the Outdoors   49
Home in a Parking Garage   53
Shaky Leg   57
Parallel Synchronicity   61
How to Remember 9/11   65
Lessons from Couchsurfers in Lafayette   69

Part Three: Austin   75

Sharing Meals   77
Hot Wax and Self Doubt   83
You Fancy the Women Folk?   85
No Second Chances   91
Watching Bats   93
Fingered   97
Last Night in Austin   101
Texas Tiny Houses   105

Part Four: West Texas   111

A Walk in My Wilderness   113
Desert Frolic   121
Hitting the Wall   127
Change of Plans, Fort Stockton   131
Bullshit and Beer   137
Prairie Man and Glamping   145
Real Men Cry   153
She Works Hard for the Money   159

Part Five: New Mexico   163

New Mexico: The Land of…Panic?   165
Expensive Taxi, Panic, and Santa Fe Miracles   173
Kindness Is Always Possible   181
Netflix Sex   185
There is Still Work to be Done   189
Wishbone and Santa Fe Spirits   193
No, Thank You   201
Last Day in Santa Fe   209
The Four-Point U-Turn   213

Dear Reader

I hope you read this book to the end and it inspires you to live a gutsy life. I want you to know that every day, you are entering a new moment to be brave. At Starbucks and spin class, you can be gutsy—courageous, even.

Gutsy is a state of being. It is the way you show up, to act with your guts, cultivating an air of moxie—this is the mark of a life well lived. You will fuck up, probably very hard. Harder than I did. But you will be able to say, even while blood is spurting and tears are falling, that you lived hard.

And that's the whole damn thing of it. The heart of the matter is that life wants you to live her. She wants you to make love to her so strongly that she forgets where and who she is. She just knows the present moment, and that it feels dramatically brave.

Be gutsy. Live hard. Speak truth.

- Traci

Disclaimer

This book describes true events of my life. I relied on old journals, text messages, emails, and recollection of events to write this book. All names and some identifying details of individuals and organizations have been changed to protect their privacy. Everything else is true and accurate to the best of my ability.

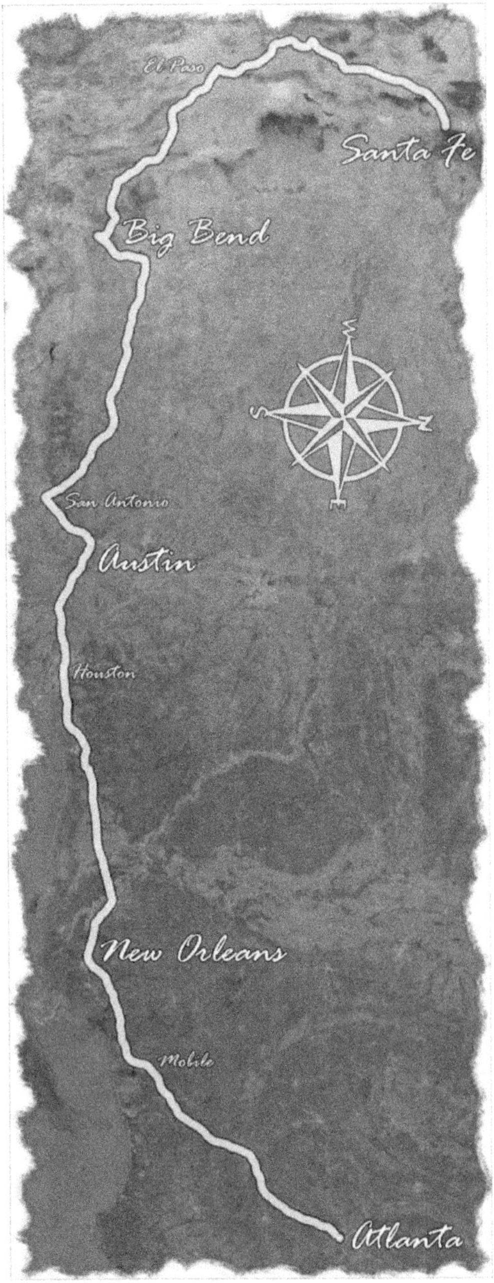

El Paso
Santa Fe
Big Bend
San Antonio
Austin
Houston
New Orleans
Mobile
Atlanta

Part One: New Orleans

Show me how big your brave is.
- Sarah Bareilles

TRACI ANN

Dear Steph

08.21.14

"Steph, can we go over to the trailer to talk?" I asked, fidgeting my palms together at my stomach. My volume increased. "I need this meeting to be very private."

"Ah, yeah." Steph looked up from her computer, somewhat startled. She tossed her half-eaten egg salad in the garbage as we walked out the office door and toward the dingy white trailer. I walked ahead of her, keenly aware of the August heat and my trembling hands.

The frigid air of the trailer hit my face abruptly as I opened the door. We sat down opposite each other at the oversized dark brown table. An uncomfortable silence hovered. Steph grabbed a pencil, opened her notebook, and scribbled the date and my name.

Traci, 8-21-14

"Steph, I know this was supposed to be a meeting about my goals moving forward with the program," I said, making sure to grab the floor first. "But there are other things I need to say to you."

"Okay," she replied, dropping the pencil. Our brown eyes locked for a silent second. I pulled my phone out of my pocket and opened the note I'd written the night before. "I wrote out what I wanted to say to you today, so please just listen."

Steph nodded, crossing her arms. And I spoke.

Steph,

I want to preface this letter by saying that this is really hard for me to say. I needed to write it in order to clearly express my points. This is a letter about work; all things said are independent of our personal relationship.

After a period of discernment, I realize I can no longer work for the New Orleans Recreation Program. I am growing at an astronomical rate and this job no longer suits my needs.

When I left this summer to work for Global Treks in Costa Rica, I was hopeful I would return refreshed for NORP. I want desperately for this to be the case, because I love my students and my work, but it is not. My two summers working for Global Treks have given me an interesting vantage point. At Global Treks, I am surrounded by powerful men and women who serve to lift me up with positive words, trusting ears, and affirming actions. At NORP, I feel the opposite; my co-workers are negative toward me. This negativity has come in the form of sexual harassment, verbal bullying, and, most recently, unwanted sexual advances from Marcus. His unsolicited, repetitive flirtation toward me has made me feel uncomfortable at work and has severely damaged our relationship. At NORP I feel scared to fully be myself, and I recognize this as very emotionally taxing. I am a talented, intelligent woman who is very good at her job, and I deserve to work beside others in mutual respect.

Another large factor affecting my choice to move forward from NORP is the standard that seems to be the norm here. I am disappointed because I value excellence in any sort of work I do. At NORP, I feel the standard set forth has been mediocrity. Continued examples of this include disrespect for work equipment, constant early departures disregarded by fellow staff members, unequal investment in actual work/programming, and cell phone use at inappropriate times. Because there is very low accountability, I do not feel compelled to invest myself fully into my work. This is not a healthy way to lead such important work with children.

I feel all of this information is necessary to speak, as it is my personal truth, as well as concrete examples of how NORP can strive to grow. There are systemic problems, which I have already mentioned. People need to be let go. I need to acknowledge that my talents are not being used to their fullest extent here, and life is very short. My hope is that this letter sheds light on areas of improvement so NORP can grow in a way that attracts educators for the long term. That is what the students need, as well as your small staff—cohesion and stability.

My voice quivered and my lower lip began to shake uncontrollably.

I want to work in a healthier environment, where I am appreciated for who I am, and empowered. I love outdoor education and value its holistic way of forming well-rounded human beings. Please know that this decision does not come from a vindictive or spiteful place; I need to make this choice for my emotional health and well-being.

Thank you for all you have given me at work including the technical skills to lead in an outdoor setting, and the soft skills to help students turn inward. I am very grateful to have worked with such wonderful children, in a stunning physical environment. In the near future I wish to speak with you about our personal relationship going forward. Know that I will continue to support you as a person, and your family. This is my two weeks' notice for NORP. Thank you for listening to me.

I clicked the top of my phone, set it on the table, and looked up at Steph. Tears had built up a glass wall inside of her eyes; she stared at the middle of the table for a long time. I sniffled back a few tears, trying to stay strong. This was never how it was supposed to play out.

Steph flicked her head down once, stood up, and inched around the table at me. I stood up to meet her, not sure what would happen next.

"I love you, and I am sorry you feel this way," she said, wrapping me in a hug. Her hug was so different than our normal hugs; this one was filled with obligation, heavy as lead. Our energies avoided each other. "Take the weekend and let's both think of how to navigate your final two weeks of work," she said, one hand still on my shoulder.

"Okay," I murmured.

As we exited, the trailer door slammed shut behind us. The walk back across the grass to the main office was short but awkward. Steph veered right back into the office, and I got into my burning hot car.

Just like that, my job was gone.

Steely Intention
08.28.14

Being sexually harassed at work is the pits. But you know what sucks balls even harder than my co-workers' asinine comments about women? Eating Lean Cuisines alone at age 28 and having a pity party due to the fear of the unknown. Life is way too short to wait and hide. I have never been one to wait around and not act.

Fuck 'em all. The contents of the recycling bin rattled as I chucked the empty Swedish meatball container in. That night, in the lamp-lit kitchen alone, I made a pledge to myself. I took an oath of steely intention:

No more Lean Cuisines alone in a home that is not mine.

No more being quiet when others say hurtful things. I will not stay in a place past its expiration date any longer. I have nothing to prove to anyone; the only judgment is between the Universe and I.

I am leaving New Orleans. This is the last page in a five-year-old chapter. Time for a huge life change. I need clarity and I am brave; a woman filled with scrappy intention. I want to go west and search for more life-giving outdoor work. I want the mountains, the desert sky, and the opportunity to teach children in a bigger wilderness.

I just resigned from my job; I have nowhere to be, and everywhere to go. I am going to pack up my car and drive to Atlanta, stay with my dear friend Heather. I will bring a map and plan my trip west from there. Paper map, internal compass, that's all I need.

"Because I can" is the only reason I need. I want so much more out of this life than eating frozen dinners in a temporary home. I want to be surrounded by incredible people, not assholes.

It is time to start anew.

The lamp-lit kitchen received my pledge with dignity and silent grace, save for the hum of the fridge.

It is time to be free.

TRACI ANN

Baton Rouge Freedom Cry

08.29.14

My cell phone drilled the wooden nightstand with an intermittent vibration. By the third round, my fingers found the phone and I pressed it to my ear.

"Hello?" I said. I cleared my throat, unsure who was at the other end, as the number was blocked.

"Good morning, Miss Traci, this is Cindy Lawrence, the director of Human Resources for the Office of State Parks," she replied.

Her strong tone woke me up fast. I had only submitted the formal written complaint yesterday.

"Good morning," I said. I twisted out of the bed sheets and put my glasses on.

"I received your written complaint regarding the harassment issues at NORP, and frankly, I'm floored." Her voice softened as she continued, "Sweetheart these are big issues you wrote about, which we have a zero tolerance for within the State."

"Yes, they are big issues. I resigned last week," I said.

"Traci, in light of the severity of your written complaint, we really need you to come to Baton Rouge and speak about all of this in person."

Adrenaline flushed my system. *Finally, a chance to be heard by someone who will do something!*

"I would be more than happy to come out," I said with conviction.

"Are you free this afternoon to meet with me and our HR specialist?" Cindy asked.

"Yes, absolutely, I can be there by one," I said.

"Great, one is fine. We will see you then. Oh and, if you can, please print out any copies of online conversations you had with Marcus. We will need all of this for the future internal investigation at NORP." Her words sounded like freedom. *Glorious, uncensored freedom!*

"Okay, I will. See you then," I said and hung up the phone.

I scrambled into the shower in awe of what just happened. They read the complaint. The ladies of HR are taking this shit seriously. Marcus's incessant 2 a.m. text messages flashed across my brain. The uninvited romantic advances that sat in my inbox from him seared on my frontal lobe.

I now have the opportunity to tell the powerful women of human resources what actually went down at work. Today.

I ate a late breakfast and, like a warrior in a white battle chariot, I rode off into the Friday lunchtime traffic crunch, ready to yell my freedom cry. The HR office was on the third floor of an off-white state building that needed an exterior pressure washing. My armpits were already damp even before the three of us sat down at the large conference table. The blasting air conditioner turned my sweat icy cold.

"Can I have some water please?" I asked Cindy after she, I, and the HR specialist sat down.

"Of course." She left the room and returned with three mini plastic bottles.

"Whenever you are ready, feel free to tell us, in your own words, what happened during your time with NORP," Cindy said, flipping to a clean yellow page on her legal pad. The other woman, dressed in a blue pantsuit, clicked a pen and stared at me.

And so, I told them what happened. It felt fucking good. Deliciously good. Divulging all the details of the verbal beating I took over a veiled ten months was difficult and easy simultaneously. I was the captain of the *Titanic*.

Yes, I see the iceberg. Yes, I am aiming for it. Prepare to be rocked.

I told them about the day riding in the white fifteen-passenger van with three of my co-workers. Reggie tapped me on the shoulder. I turned around from the front passenger seat. He flicked his dreads behind his shoulder. "So Trace, say you were at a club, dancing with a guy, right?" he said, throwing a glace to Darrius to listen in from the back seat. Darrius plucked his ear buds from his ears and leaned forward. "Things are getting good, and he asks you back to his place. Which sex position would you use on him?" Reggie asked, uninterested in the look of terror in my eyes.

"Are you kidding me Reggie? What the fuck?" I said. We were stopped at a red light and it took everything I had not to throw his black ass out of the van.

He looked back at Darrius for a grin of encouragement. "Doggie style? Or do you like it on top? You seem like a girl who likes to be in charge." He leaned closer to my face.

His words shrunk me and I wanted to stab knives in his eyes. I turned around to face front; Marcus held the steering wheel tightly, and the final half mile we all rode in silence. That night I cried in my car for an hour before going into my overpriced rental home.

I told them about the day that Darrius cornered me in the grass parking lot after a sweaty day of teaching canoe lessons.

"Trace, you be looking all sexy in that tight red mini skirt on your Instagram, you dress that way all the time outside of work?" he asked suggestively, all 6'2" of him engulfing me in fear as I tried to unlock the door to my Chevy faster.

"I like to look nice." I said, feigning confidence. Everyone else had left for the day, and being along with him drew my stomach into a knot.

"I bet you get down in that skirt." He leaned to the side of me, trying to look at my ass. "Mmm, bet you dance *real* good…"

I got into my car and drove off without a word. I wanted to puke.

I told them about the times I went to my boss and confided in her. She said she would talk to the guys and fill out complaints to HR. She delivered a prompt monologue about the importance of respect in the workplace at our quarterly staff development day over a catered lunch. When the updated videos on workplace sexual harassment were issued from the Office of State Parks, she made us all watch them immediately. I remember feeling confident that with her filing the complaints and us watching the videos, the tension would break.

Cindy shifted in her chair in the office uncomfortably. She pushed a manila folder across the brown conference table at me, the other HR lady looked at me sadly. I opened the folder and found one paper in it from Steph, with an obscure note, about the incident in the van. It was vague, and no specific names were written, except mine.

"This is all the paperwork she filed all year?" I asked, noticing the cold sweat was now present on my back.

"Yes, this is all we ever received from her since last fall." Cindy looked at me empathetically.

Claws of rage tore apart my insides; my world imploded in betrayal.

Boats were rocked. Tears were shed. Jobs were lost. Good thing I worked at a place with life vests. Too bad the life vests couldn't preserve my co-workers' souls, even if their bodies died in the sea of my truthful words.

Sink, bitches.

I sang it. I yelled it. I pounded the evidence out of my chest. I did it because I needed to move forward. I needed the outdated, quiet person inside of me to die. She was already bloodied from being dragged across the gravel of employment abuse. *Just let her die. There is a new woman inside just waiting to jump on stage.*

Four hours later, the two HR women stopped scribbling on their notepads and shook my hand firmly. "Thank you for coming forward with this, we will move swiftly with an internal investigation. You are brave and you are heard, Traci." They held open the double doors to the lobby for me. "No man or woman should have to go through what you just did. We will make sure it never happens again at NORP, okay?" Cindy said.

"Yes ma'am, thank you," I said, pressing the elevator button.

"Good luck in your future endeavors. Stephanie just lost one hell of an employee, and I'm really sorry we did too." She stepped back and let the elevator doors close between us.

The traffic on the way back to New Orleans was heavy, but my heart was lighter. *I can do anything now.*

There is a poem that speaks of how one lives in the Tao (the Way):
Go where you are sent
Wait until you are shown what to do
Act with whole self
Walk away with empty hands

I reclaimed my power today in Baton Rouge. I spoke my own rendering of the Tao poem to the traffic.

Fly home to New Orleans
Realize Titanic problems are always meant to sink to murky depths
Aim Titanic into that cold, pointy motherfucker
Jump in my lifeboat and row away without looking back

Oh…and also enjoy a four-day weekend in New Orleans, doing the things I love.

TRACI ANN

Rainy with a Chance of Brass
8.30.14

My plans of stealing New Orleans away for one last torrid dance in between the humid sheets were sabotaged by strong summer rains. I woke up to the tin roofs draining thunderstorm after thunderstorm into the street. Instead, I enjoyed Bayou St. John from the comfort of my incredibly transitory house-sitting spot on Delgado Street. I perched myself at the breakfast table, facing the open backdoor, and watched the rain come down. My muse wandered around on the internet with coffee as its companion.

Tiny home ideas were the brainstorm of Saturday morning and into the rainy afternoon. Apparently tiny homes, small homes the size of parking lot spaces built on trailers, are a thing. As hip as kale in the Bywater or Cider Week in Astoria, tiny home websites were scattered across the internet. In the YouTube videos I watched, most builders of the homes wore skinny jeans and hipster glasses. Building my own small, solar home had become a dream of mine. It grew out of living in all sorts of dwellings in my early twenties and being exhausted with shitty landlords. I researched and dreamt of building my own tiny home, even if it meant I had to wear skinny jeans and eat kale.

By evening the rain stopped and the sun painted the wet bayou sky with a silky orange, fading to dark blue. I put on a pair of jeans, a black Saints t-shirt that hugged my athletic build, and took to the French Quarter for my original plan of the day—to do the things I loved in New Orleans, and end it on a good note.

Success was achieved. I always forget that, no matter what, there is always a festival in New Orleans. As I rounded the bricked corner of St. Ann and Bourbon, for that one last glance at Bourbon Street's craziness, I remembered it was Southern Decadence weekend.

Oh no. Oh yes.

So many banana-hammocks decorated with pink feathers, so many lesbians in costume, so much pounding house music, so much free love. I took in a block of the love, and then, feeling overwhelmed as I always do on Bourbon, I ducked back towards the river. Wondering if my recent lust for bi-sexuality was genuine, I began to admire women on my walk to the river. I looked up to a crowded, dimly lit balcony of all ladies partying. Two lady couples were kissing strongly, eyes closed, both holding cocktail glasses at their side. I had never kissed a woman, so I couldn't be sure whether I would like it or not. Nothing of huge value surfaced in the way of sexuality epiphanies, so I continued on my adventure, remaining straight.

I followed the curve of the river, lovely as a lady's hips, down to Frenchmen Street for some good old brass music. The walk along the Mississippi was as sublime and romantic as always; the skyline's lights made parts of the river dance in illumination. Huge freighters floated silently towards the bridge and the distant sound of coffee mugs being cleared off a table at Café Du Monde permeated my awareness.

I stopped in the Blue Nile Bar for a drink and Washboard Chaz was snapping out a catchy number on his washboard with metal fingers. I realized suddenly that this was the same bar that I sat in the very first night I moved to the city, nearly five years ago.

Life is a circle.

I downed a fierce Jack and coke, went back out onto Frenchmen Street, and trailed a trumpet sound through the puddles until I located its source. The sound of a brass horn is my second favorite sound in the world. My first is the sound of the Pacific Railroad train cars screeching through town on the local tracks.

I found the brass sound and sat at the bar for a full set. Nothing soothes my soul like moving to the sound of that brass. I swayed in my seat, feeling too sublime to dance in the front with the other people.

So good. So good.

A few men washed ashore near my barstool with sweet, meager pick-up lines: "You here all alone, sweetheart?" or "You think I'm cute, right?"

Baby, you have NO idea what I just went through. Step off.

I sipped my Abita calmly, and let the trumpet be my pop-off.

Satisfied with the evening, I jumped in my white Impala and drove home.

"Thanks for a great night, baby," I whispered into New Orleans' thick black arms. We kissed and I fell asleep.

TRACI ANN

Sunday Funday
08.30.14

I think every Sunday should be filled with things that make you ecstatic. Screw doing the laundry, screw your lover instead. Make the groceries? Make love, not groceries, baby.

My Sunday was super fun. A mysterious man who I see from time to time in New Orleans, who we will call Justin, whisked me off to a late brunch. He has a grin a mile wide and this sexy entrepreneur flair I adore. High fives and belly laughter were the first orders of business as we recounted tales of the summer—his trip to Australia for the band he manages, and my recent stand for women and workplace social justice.

"Trace, I am so proud of you! Those guys sound like assholes and you deserve to work in an amazing environment." Justin kissed me on the cheek. "So, when will they do the internal investigation at NORP?" he asked.

"Not sure, they seemed pretty adamant about doing it soon though," I said, taking a swig of my bottomless mimosa. "I will probably be in Atlanta by then, though. I gotta get out of here, wanna start over…" I trailed off.

"Trace, you lead such a massive life!" He laughed, and squeezed my knee under the table. He raised his glass for a toast. "To you, for being brave, wonderful, and to fresh starts!"

We chipped our mimosa glasses together and feasted on eggs benedict.

I loved Sundays spent with this guy.

After brunch we decided to meditate. I had never tried this form of meditation. It involved lots of steamy kisses and dewy grass dancing underneath my bare legs. We rolled around in the park playfully, the way you do when you are so grounded in a moment that nothing matters and everything matters all at once. We kissed, embraced, laughed, and wondered if the meditation was working. I knew I felt calmer. We never dated officially during the two years I knew Justin, we just meditated.

We stopped kissing for a minute and he lifted me on top of him. We sat facing each other, my tanned legs straddling him. "So when are you leaving for Atlanta then?" he asked, brushing the excess grass from my orange shorts.

"Tuesday," I said, pressing my hips flush against his. I wanted him so bad. Right there, in the park, in front of any person who wanted to pass by.

"You should definitely come by my place before you leave," he replied. He kissed me again, biting my tongue playfully. For a split second I thought about staying in New Orleans, just so we could continue our meditation practices. We caught each other's gaze for a long moment, not saying anything. His eyes were always so genuine, never wanting more than to see me happy.

"I want to be happy, Justin. Something inside of me says to go west. After Atlanta I want to go west," I said. "I can feel it inside of me…like a call to greatness. Does that make sense?"

"Yes, absolutely." He nodded, the way a fellow seeker nods. He knew what I meant. "Go live that massive life Trace. The world needs your greatness," he said, grinning, holding my face in his hands.

God, if all men were created equal—well, we most likely wouldn't grow or learn a lot. Amen to the evolved and non-evolved men. Y'all serve the world in different ways.

Storage Unit
9.1.14

I have a storage unit on St. Charles Avenue in New Orleans. When storage units first became a thing, I couldn't understand it. Why would anyone have enough stuff or a reason to place their beloved things in a locked up dark prison? It is like the bad part of *Toy Story 2* when Andy goes off to college and the toys get left on the curbside. Horrific.

Well, I have one. It contains all my beloved items of this human life. Most of it is salvaged wooden furniture, a queen-sized mattress, trinkets, clothing, dumpster finds, and my UFC pink boxing gloves. There are other, more domesticated things as well: a set of flatware from an ex-boyfriend, silverware, pots and pans, blue measuring cups my mom gave me for Christmas, and my prized martini glassware. Everything is boxed up and impeccably stacked, like I won a game of life-sized Tetris. Someday, I vow, these items will live in a functional shelter that I call my home. Until this occurs, I pay $80 per month for Public Storage to house my belongings.

I went to the unit today to grab another bag of clothing for this week's impending, life-boggling trip. I am getting the hell out of dodge. Atlanta is my starting point; I will go there, stay with my friend Heather, post up, and get some clearer headspace after the recent work crisis.

I left Public Storage with my tent, inflatable green Thermarest, Northface jacket, and a 60- liter backpack filled with cold-weather clothing. I let my gut instinct set the packing intention. No, Atlanta will not require mittens or a winter jacket…but the high desert and mountains of New Mexico will. Something deep inside of me is already in the west. I hear the tribal drum beats calling me from time to time. I packed for rain, snow, a beach—in the event that I make it all the way to California—my first solo camping trip, and possible job interviews.

If you throw enough shit at a wall, something is bound to stick.

Story of Stuff, Home, and Betty
9.2.14

I am a minimalist. As I mentioned before, all the assets I have fit in a five by ten corrugated metal storage unit. How do you know if you have accumulated more things? Try to put your minimalist amount of things into your car. They do not fit.

This is a slight exaggeration. Everything I wanted to bring fit in my car. I squeezed my three-tiered plastic shower tower behind the driver's seat. I crammed my special memory foam pillow in the remaining space in the trunk. I am planning a road trip wearing a blindfold; therefore, I reserve the right to bring all sorts of medications and variations of soap and tampons.

Waves of mania and melancholy surged over me as I packed. Packing is as familiar to me in my adult life as breathing. Traveling was the reality that dominated my early twenties. The weekend overnight trains to Paris when I lived in Italy, the seven-month backpacking trip across South America when I turned twenty-five, and countless island hopping journeys in the Caribbean. During those years I created a life rhythm that has prevailed. Pick place, pack, travel; pick place, pack, travel.

Surging happiness coursed through my veins as I admired my pack job. Then, as I looked at everything in the trunk once more, a wave of sadness, which materialized as a little girl, tugged on my shirt.

"When will we have a home?" the little inner girl asked, looking up at me from my waist. We looked very similar, though she was translucent.

I knelt down beside her, holding her pretty blue dress at the sides. "This trip is different. This is not travel. On the surface it is. We will see things, and take pictures, and meet new people. But this trip, which the universe is forcefully pushing at us, is more of a pilgrimage. We will travel within and without to find where the vibe outside matches our vibe inside. Does that make sense?" I asked.

"Kind of," she shrugged her shoulders and pouted out her little lips at me.

"I want a home too," I said out loud, to the empty parking garage, in agreement with the little girl who looked like me. "I want this trip to help us find that special place to create a sacred space," I gently cooed, trying to convince her to be on board with the trip.

"I'm scared!" she screamed, and rolled on her side, away from me, and began to cry. My stomach hurt.

I lean my head against my arms on the car. Maybe it is all a farce; maybe this is not a pilgrimage of sacred proportions. Maybe it does not matter where I go because in the end I am going to end up broke, drinking burnt black coffee at a diner in New Mexico with a server named Betty. Betty will give me a warmer and wonder why in the world I didn't just keep my cute little outdoor job with health insurance in Louisiana.

Betty's got another thing coming. *I am answering the hero's call, Betty; I am following my heart's guidance in hopes that it will lead me to a new invigorating place to call home, build a space to live, and live amongst people with similar views.*

You feeling me, Betty?

I slammed the trunk shut, its sound echoed through the empty parking garage at Public Storage. I started the car and dismissed the passing vision of doubtful Betty at the New Mexico diner.

"We will have a home soon, sweetie. No more car dressers or storage unit elevator rides. Home is near," I said to my little girl, buckling her into the backseat. When I adjusted the rearview mirror, she had disappeared.

Part Two: Atlanta

An interesting fate awaits almost everyone, mouse or man, who does not conform.
- *The Tale of Despereaux*

TRACI ANN

10 to 65 to 85
09.3.14

Yesterday I got outta dodge. I flew the coop. I pushed that gas pedal so hard. I drove away from New Orleans. I cruised on three thunderstorm-laden interstates: the I-10, I-65, and I-85 northeast into Atlanta.

Eight hours is a long time to be driving. My brain entertained a party of questions and thoughts. *What type of clouds are those? Oh shit, a thunderstorm. I wonder how good I am doing on gas mileage? How many people are masturbating right now as they drive? Has anyone on this interstate gotten road head? What about the people with all the stuff, and the fluffy dog in that Subaru, what's their story? Why do people text and drive? What do I want to eat for lunch, Chik-Fil-A or Wendy's?*

Then the big one got me. *Where are we all going?*

Once I got done with my amusing and vulgar question and answer session, and tired of shouting along to the blaring music, I settled into observing the road. Weird stuff happens on the road. Life happens on the road. I watched a lady in a beat up rusted red Sunfire, with a cracked windshield, create a light show with her brakes. My cruise control pushed her, and her man riding shotgun, in and out of my view. Every time I glanced over as we passed, interchanged into the other's life, I saw her hands in the air. Not on the wheel. She was yelling at this man beside her. Presumably telling him to get out of the car at the next exit…maybe. I couldn't hear her over my booming music and wind-rushed environment. This is what people do while they're driving? Life is so stupid. Stupid amazing. What made her so mad? Why did he sit, arms crossed, and take it? Why do we all take this life so seriously?

More of life happened on I-85, closing in on Atlanta. I was in hot pursuit of the newest part of me, when, on the other side of the interstate, life mysteriously ended for someone else.

Black body bag. Demolished car with a smashed window lying dead in the green grassy median. Semi-truck splayed out on the slick road. A four-mile line of red ants stood at attention. People stood outside their cars two miles up from the accident wondering why they needed to wait longer for Chik-Fil-A. Why did we, the cars on the opposite side, get to breeze past death?

So much. So much life is happening everywhere, all the time. It truly is very fleeting. It all matters and nothing matters. We will all die and in the end, nobody will be around to give a fuck about how you participated. But it is still your job to engage in this dramatic play called life. To live it the best you know how, until you get splayed out by a semi.

I arrived to Heather's gated apartment complex around six o'clock. It was already pitch dark, a reminder that the summer was ending. The clouds were low and the air was noticeably less humid than in New Orleans. I grabbed my overnight bag, and raced up the three flights of stairs to her apartment. I knocked on the door hard, excited to see her. She whipped open the door and I got blasted with a wafting smell of soy and stir-fry.

"Ahhh! You crazy woman, you! You made it!" She hugged me hard.

"Yeah there were a lot of storms, but the drive was fine," I replied, feeling my smile across my face.

"Your hair got really long, and you have more gray coming in!" she teased, inviting me into the house.

"Stop, I know," I smiled and covered my brown-gray locks with my hands, still in denial that I was rapidly about to join the salt-and-pepper club.

"It looks good, like a wise librarian," she laughed playfully.

Her apartment was petite and filled with three years of graduate school books, marathon bicycles, a cat tower, and a messy counter filled with mail. Heather had a cat, Cody, who I had met before. I tossed my bag on the futon and Cody came out from her bedroom, meowing.

"Cody!" I said, stroking his pretty orange fur.

"Awww, he missed you," Heather said from the kitchen. "Pour us some wine, girl," she continued, motioning to the cabinet next to the fridge. I poured us two large glasses of red wine, and we toasted to friendship, to me, to new beginnings. She cooked an amazing welcoming meal of a stir fry ensemble she had purchased off of a chef website. We ate at her glass dining room table and reminisced about the year we were roommates in New Orleans. Each story began with, "Do you remember that time we…" and ended in purifying, gut wrenching laughter.

"You know Trace, you can stay as long as you need," she said between fits of laughter, her pale complexion turning red from the story of our first very drunken night in New Orleans, when we missed the ferry ride home. "Oh my god. Can you believe we just laid down on Poydras Street, looking up at the buildings?" She was in stitches.

After dinner, I scrubbed the plates. I was on the final dish when I heard a loud metal clanking sound at my feet. Stella, Heather's overly-excited pitbull, had brought her leash to my feet.

"Ah, she knows it is time for her nighttime walk. You wanna take her with me?" Heather asked, clipping the leash to Stella's giant collar.

"Sure."

We giggled as we walked up the sidewalk. The wine made my head feel woozy; the air was refreshed from the thunderstorms. I breathed in, and noticed my chest was less tight.

TRACI ANN

Magic Bagels and Running Under Rainbows
09.4.14

Today I met Michael Bagels. That's the name I gave him in my phone. Being my first full day in Atlanta I decided to take myself out to lunch at the Einstein Bagel place. I wore a pair of skinny Levis, a pink, fitted tee I had purchased at a consignment shop, heeled boots, and my awesome floral-print snapback, which reads, "Because I Can" in big, white-and-black lettering. This, unofficially, became my woman battle cry ever since the resignation. The pitch for my haters goes something like this:

Ask me why, bitch?

To which I promptly stick my finger up at my hat.

Because I can. Boom.

Then I walk away like a badass.

I stepped up to the counter and Michael took my order for a turkey bacon avocado on an Asiago bagel, and noticed the hat.

"Killer hat!" he said with a huge smile, layering turkey on the sandwich.

"Thanks!" I stood proudly wearing my motto, grateful I didn't need to try out the badass pitch.

I must have looked out of place because his next question was, "Where are you from?"

I guess Atlanta natives do not wear snapbacks with brazen messages on them.

A rush of embarrassment and sadness flushed my cheeks. *Where am I from?* Since I dropped New Orleans like a bad habit two days ago, it felt like cheating, but I said it anyway: "New Orleans."

He was over the moon, as are most people when I say I am from there. Romanticized stories surface: "Ah yeah, the jazz..." or "That one Mardi Gras..." Yes, I know. I know what it means to miss New Orleans. However, Michael had a different connection.

"From what I do know about my mama, she was a dancer in New Orleans," he said.

I sat down to my glorious bagel of freedom-from-the-afternoon-rain. Michael sauntered over to the nearby beverage station and half-shouted to me, "How long are you in Atlanta? You should check out Little Five Points, there is really cool art and graffiti there…you seem like a girl who likes her art."

He piqued my interest. I *am* an artist, and love street art.

Keep talking, Mike—I'm listening.

I tried to feel out his vibe; after being so wounded from my co-workers, I was compelled to be suspicious around well-intentioned men. Was he just suggesting random things in hopes to get me on a date?

I took the leap. "Well I resigned from my job…so I am not sure how long I will be here. I do love art."

Michael stopped polishing the coffee canisters and burst into excitement. "You should definitely go to Little Five Points, then! In fact, let me get your number so I could bring you there or something."

At that same moment I saw his ringed finger. A repeat of the married-man incident? *No. No thank you, absolutely not.* Marcus' dark hands entered my awareness. His dark, strong hands, with the silver wedding band.

Marcus and I sat across from each other at the small coffee table that butted up against the side wall of the work office. It was four in the afternoon and everyone had departed for the day. I had planned this meeting with Marcus, asking him to stay at work with me later so we could speak privately. We had just finished putting the canoes away, and both of our shirts were covered in August's tropical moisture.

"Marcus, I wanted to talk to you in person about all of this. The text messages in June. How you confessed your feelings for me. I was overwhelmed back then. I asked you to stop, thanked you for your honesty, and thought we were good. Why did you keep texting me?" My feet tapped nervously, angrily.

"Trace, what I did was wrong, I know. I am sorry. I don't know what else to do, though!" He held up his hands for a moment in defense. "I'm sorry I started texting you again when you were away this summer.

I missed you. But I know that's no excuse." Marcus spoke quietly, cupping his big hands between his knees.

"Marcus! This is insane! You don't know what else to do?" I hissed.

"No! I said I was sorry for my behavior. What else do you want from me?" Our eyes locked. We locked eyes so often in the past year. Too many to count. That kind of eye-locking where you glimpse the other person's soul. Every other time it felt loving, kind, and open. Today our eyes locked in rage, betrayal, and wrongful lust. I forced myself not to feel any attraction to him.

"I want you to stop this behavior," I said. "Stop saying you are sorry and then continuing the actions. This is fucking crazy. You are married, with two children. I do not have feelings for you and never pursued you." My voice was firm. "I used to love to come to work, to work with you. Now, I hate it—I can't stand to even be around you!" My body shook with anger and sadness.

We argued in circles for a few more rounds, both feeling shittier by the second. I knew it was over. Marcus pushed me to my breaking point.

It was the last conversation we had before I left.

Michael was standing next to my table now, with the cleaning rag in his married-man hand. There was something different in his eyes, a childish enthusiasm. He was on the vibe, the vibe of human connectedness and spiritual flow. He didn't want to cheat on his wife with me, he just wanted to help me have a nice time in Atlanta.

"I write poetry, do you know of any places I can go to read some of it, and listen?" I asked.

"Yes! Do you really write? There is this spoken-word thing that happens at The Java Monkey, and you should totally check it out. Also, I'm trying to get together musicians and poets who want to collaborate on, like, consciousness-based hip-hop music. If you want, I could send you my music samples and you could write over them."

I wrote down the address of the poetry reading, Michael's email address, and took a bite of my bagel. I buzzed with happy energy. Michael departed to take out the trash, but not before giving me a neat lineup of music I had never heard of. I basked in the magnificence of magic bagels and enjoyed feeling a bit more in flow than I had in a while.

Ancient teachings say that when the student is ready the teacher appears. To which I reply: how many teachers do we all get to have?

What is better than magic bagels and new age-y baristas? Trying out a running group with my soul sister Heather!

Tonight we went to an adventure run, a three-mile journey that took us all over Atlanta on foot. Adventure is my middle name, so I was stoked—but adventure turned to bait-and-switch torture once I remembered Atlanta has hills, and I do not run for pleasure. It was all fun until I caught some serious running cramps. I made it a lame mile and a half before I caught a solid one in my right side and had to stop. Heather waited for me, jogging in place. The group of quick-dry clad runners scooted around a corner.

"I'm sorry, I can't run anymore," I gasped out, and then laughed at myself.

"No worries, we can just walk back," she replied, turning off her fancy marathon-runner watch.

We turned around and headed back the way we came. Then it began to pour. We walked. We ran. We laughed. We also got very turned around and lost. I always forget to *not* listen to her navigation because it is never correct. She stared at me sheepishly when we had effectively walked in a circle within a well-kept grove of ritzy houses.

I told her I wouldn't have it any other way on a Thursday night in September. I meant it.

We finally found the main road and passed over the railroad tracks near a Dairy Queen. We were drenched in sun shower rain and the air smelled pungently fresh.

She gasped. "Look at that rainbow! There are two, there are always two!" She pointed vigorously to the sky. Above our sweaty hot mess of a run were two gorgeous rainbows, so stunning that people were pulling off the road to get out of their cars and snap photos of it. I found it funny that the rainbow began at a brewery and ended caressing the roof of the Dairy Queen. How sacred.

Just when you think humanity is a collective zombie, it floors you in the form of people acting like children in awe and wonder of the natural world.

Even though my legs harbored a sensation akin to rubbery sledge hammers, I would say my introduction to the subculture of local running groups was exceeded by rainbow beauty and fueled by Michael and his soul-enriching bagels.

TRACI ANN

Ode to the Outdoors
9.5.14

I woke up feeling odd. Shitty, actually. I got up, stretched, and made myself a healthy breakfast of eggs, avocado, and some grapes. I placed the colorful plate in front of me at Heather's table and just stared at it for a solid fifteen minutes. Edgy anxiety and irritation wafted all around me. Heather had suggested the night before that I take a long walk to clear my head on one of the many wooded PATH trails that run all throughout the city. The idea of a hike lifted my spirits just enough for me to consume the vibrant plate of food.

I headed out the door around noon, the sun brightly shining, yet the morning's anxiety hadn't burned off. It welled up underneath my skin. *Why the hell am I in Atlanta?* Ego and grief seemed to lurk just around every bend of the trail.

The hike was lovely and needed. The damp leaves welcomed my feet and my backpack was a comforting weight on my back. Each step further into the green abyss, more and more anxiety diffused from my open pores and in the vast air. I admired a slowly moving stream below a bridge, listened to the orchestra of birds singing for a gorgeous day, and stopped every so often to look up and notice the tips of the trees coyly hinting at fall. I hiked a few miles out, emerging at a baseball field across town. I ate a trail picnic of apples, carrots, and granola, chewing slowly, savoring the flavor and the moment.

On the return loop, new, more productive questions surfaced. *How do I know what to go after in my adult life to make me happy?* The answer followed promptly, voiced by an inner source. *Just look at your childhood. Everything you did as a child is the key to the present and beyond.*

Growing up, I was such a tom-boy. I was the only girl in a ragtag crew of six neighborhood boys, one of whom was my little brother. We all touted Nerf guns, rode on mountain bikes, went go-carting in the fall, and crafted snow shelters in the winter. I shredded everyone in pickup basketball and was the leader in planning our yearly winter and summer forts in the woods. My brother and I would take to the power line trails on our four-wheelers with imagination, eating the summer air for lunch. Our mother would call us in for dinner and we would recount the progress of the stick built lean-to or the new four-wheeler trail we had discovered. I remember those days so clearly; I was such a happy kid, so connected to the outside world. I didn't give a damn about Barbies or anything remotely girlie. I was the queen of the New York State outdoor club and all the boys were my court.

When asked what their favorite sensation is, all women respond differently. To some women it might be the sexy feel of a new pair of pumps, or the feminine prowess you sense when you make your man sigh in delight as you pleasure him. For me it is the sensation of snow below the boots: crunchy, layered, muted and complex. The best is a walk at midnight in a fresh downpour of silent snow that is tinted pink from ambient light. Nothing feels or smells better to me than anything in this world. Yes, you can smell snow.

Why, then, did it take me until almost age thirty to reclaim my love for the natural world?

I am a woman who likes to be outdoors. Although there are entire big box stores and outfitters condoning being outside, a lot of women don't jump on the granola train. At least not many of my east-coast friends I used to roll with. The woman I used to be did not know she was destined for the outdoors. She lost touch with it. Somewhere between puberty and college I was convinced that business suits and fast cars were much sexier than flannels and a bicycle. Before I reconsidered honing my innate outdoor goddess, I equated the wilderness to be simply that—a place wildly inaccessible and definitely not suitable for a budding marketing graduate to hang out in. Men like women who wear make-up and put out on the first date, not strong women who want to help pitch the tent, let alone go camping with them.

After today's hike in the local wilderness of Atlanta I reclaimed my adult alignment with everything that is flannel, recycled, and about leaves. I am a lady who loves her natural world. I love to be dirty, I enjoy how my own body smells once it is two showers removed from society. I have a burning need to live mostly outside right now. I try so hard to be happy inside, but it feels so foreign and incorrect. Nothing gives me more balance than the weight of a backpack with all of my living essentials neatly packed inside.

The sweat on my body felt incredible as I peeled off my hiking clothes in Heather's bathroom. I admired my naked body fresh off the trail. I glistened, smelled of trees, and my legs looked more tanned. Although still uncertain of my future, I did feel refreshed, and noticeably less anxious than when I'd set out midday. I watched the grime of the urban trail wash down my thighs and into the drain, and turned up the shower extra hot.

The hike confirmed obvious things about my life as it stands. I must be outside every day in a large way. I must look into my childhood for my adulthood destiny.

The anxiety of the unknown still fluttered around me like an annoying small piece of paper that got stuck in the A/C vent. It rattled in the background, and when I took my heart off the present moment, I hear the flickering sound of paper against metal. It was the sound of unemployment and a broken heart for the city I once loved.

If I can just be here now, enjoy each moment as it unfolds, I will not hear the rattling paper stuck in the vent.

TRACI ANN

Home in a Parking Garage

09.7.14

I wanted to pee in excitement, to pass out in a delirium of happiness.

Why? I toured my first tiny house yesterday with Heather.

I noticed alternative living a few years back, but only this year have I taken the idea of living in something other than a rickety rental or massive McMansion seriously. Enter, the tiny home. It is exactly what the words imply—homes the size of a RV, made of whatever the hell you want, either on a trailer or stuck in the ground.

Heather and I went to a tour of a SCADpad—a group of experimental housing units that were the size of one parking space each—inside of a parking garage, designed and created by the students from the Savannah College of Arts and Design. Each one was artistically maddening. Multi-colored vintage yard sticks covered the entire floor of the American-themed pad, while torn fabric hung abstractly from the ceiling of the European-inspired one. Copper colanders mounted upside down acted as the shades for each light bulb and the lofted sleeping area looked so cozy. Heather climbed up the one-foot-wide staircase, which contained stylish dresser drawers below it, to the loft. She flopped down on her back, looking up at the strips of fabric close to her face.

"I am so glad you surprised me with this adventure, Trace," she said, batting at the fabric like a cat.

"Me too," I replied, snapping photo after photo of the parts of the tiny home that inspired me.

Once we finished exploring all of the SCADpads, we joined the ten other tiny-home enthusiasts who sat in the community area chatting about building codes in various cities and what each of our pipe-dream dwellings might look like.

"I definitely want to use reclaimed barn wood on mine," Tina, the farmer from South Carolina, said.

"Well I want to do mine up fully solar, and then I'd love to have a garden too," a burly bald man spoke from the opposing couch.

A tsunami of gratitude and happiness knocked over any previous ideas of who I was and what I wanted from this life. We all sat on the fourth floor of a parking garage in the heart of Atlanta, a spray-painted orange tire with a glass top as our coffee table, framing the lively conversation. Hanging out with this crew of fellow tiny-home enthusiasts was wild. We all came from our own stories up until now, but the story we wanted to tell, going forward, was inextricably linked. We wanted to tell a story of collaboration and community, of using space more intentionally to create functional and gorgeous shelters.

Words raced into my brain to try and process what was happening as I witnessed a new piece of my life. I have found my people. I was frenzied and happy, like a pinball machine on its bonus round. *Sold.* I want to create my tiny home yesterday! I heard sirens going off in my head, people seemed to be yelling from the neighboring rooftops, and the heavens cracked open above the tiny home mecca I had located. Everything gasped one, singular, orgasmic, "Yes!" The angels whispered in my ear, "This is for you, please build one soon."

Okay, maybe a choir of angels didn't show up, but the swell of joy I felt in my heart was pretty much akin to my perception of angelic choirs.

If the tiny homes themselves did not strike me enough, what floored me was Heather's openness to the whole thing. I brought her to the parking garage under no instructions other than that she was coming with me on an adventure. Watching her unravel her own questions of her belongings, their true worth, and the price she pays for her current life. It was brilliant.

"So what do you think of this whole parking lot house thing your friend brought you to?" Will said to Heather, wagging his finger at me. Will was the organizer of the SCADpad meetup.

"I mean, it really makes me think, what do I actually need?" Heather replied, pointing both her knees at Will. "I have two marathon bikes in my house, and furniture I barely use. What's the point?" Will nodded his head in agreement.

Could Heather live tiny? Could we all live in smaller physical homes and then expand into the truest version of ourselves that we are meant to inhabit?

Society is a mean bitch. Tricking everyone into the American value meal. Kids, a mortgage, and your daily Xanax. It was invigorating to connect with others who were not drinking the Kool-Aid that has long since been spiked with fear.

That night, after Heather went to sleep with Stella and Cody in her bed, I sat awake on the futon with my journal, and I wrote a love letter.

Dear future tiny home,

I adore you. I want you on wheels so we can continue to explore this world. Europe, India, Canada. Shit, I didn't think of bringing you to Barcelona. Perhaps you will be a submarine with retractable wheels?

I am saying yes to building you, dear tiny home. Once you are built I want to teach others to build as well. I want to form a tiny home commune with all my fellow crystal-healing, Reiki-loving, energy-buzzing hippie friends.

I will build you not for power, not for money, or fame. None of that is important to this new emerging version of myself. I want gutsy freedom from outdated norms, and to balance all parts of my life.

Love, your excited future inhabitant,
Traci

TRACI ANN

Shaky Leg
09.7.14

Palms sweaty. Legs shaking involuntarily.

I spread them in a wider stance, hoping it would be less painful. I had never really tried this position. The lights blasted my body with heat. I kept my clothes on to start, just to leave them wanting a little more. I giggled all over my insides and let others watch the act.

I read a poem out loud. In front of fifty people in a balmy coffeehouse courtyard in Atlanta. One of my original pieces of art. I want to publish my poetry like I want to eat chocolate during my period; it is a ravenous desire that comes on strong and needs to be quenched.

Therefore, in an effort to support my poetic desires, I thought of a fun idea. Why not find a spoken word night in every city I stop during this road trip and read my poems? I needed to keep myself afloat. An outlet, to use as a reminder, when I am feeling low, that I am not my previous job. I am a badass writer-queen who has a booming voice that must be heard.

We are all inherently strong people, and to stand inside of ourselves during the scariest storms is the truest test of strength. You say you are a fucking warrior? Well here is the sinkhole beneath your feet. I dare you not to scream.

I didn't scream. I just scrambled through the crowd at the Java Monkey and scribbled my full name on the open mic sheet. I was number eleven. Plenty of time to sit next to Heather and channel courage. The stage was small, the dimensions of an elevator floor, covered in black carpeting. There was one mic, a borrowed music stand, and a battered wooden stool. Heather sipped her Frappuccino beside me. The lights in the courtyard behind us dimmed, leaving the elevator stage blasted in white light. The host, a tall old man with a gray afro, stepped onto the stage.

"Welcome to the Java Monkey open mic night, y'all!" he said, and the crowd applauded. "Alright! First up, Traci Ann. I don't like to do these things in order," he said, his hands shaking with a bit of Parkinson's.

Shit. Exposed. No time. Sinkhole. Hurry! Channel inner badass writer-queen.

I looked at the floor in front of my seat, pretending I had no idea who Traci Ann was. Heather nudged me sweetly. "You got this! C'mon, get up there!"

"Traci Ann, do we have a Traci Ann in the house?" he asked into the microphone once more. I stood up suddenly, feeling fifty eyes linger on my body in the dim light of the seats. The host looked at me, pleased I had the balls to stand up.

"Looks like we got a first timer," he said.

"New *shiiiiit*," the crowd hooted into the darkness with unexpected unison. I made my way to the aisle.

"Where ya from sweetie?" gray-haired afro-man asked.

"New Orleans," I replied.

"They didn't do too well against our birds today," he smiled at me, turning over the mic.

I unfolded the typed poem I'd brought and read it all the way through. My legs shook harder than they had during the best full-body orgasm I've ever experienced. Heather recorded the whole thing on her iPhone. It was my third time reading in front of a crowd. The applause at the end was secondary. The way I felt speaking was a welcome release of lifeblood into a microphone I was too short for.

Revisiting your writing by reading it aloud, by performing it, is directly placing yourself back into your life moments. Your voice rattles in the same place that it did when you were upset on that Tuesday afternoon. Your passion for the event booms against the mic. When you visit your art after it has been birthed, it is like visiting the son you put up for adoption. He grew tall, not totally what you expected, but still you are proud and really confused about him.

Proud, confused, and a nervous mama I was tonight. Step one on my poetry publication quest, done.

Before Heather and I disappeared back onto the streets of Decatur

I bought a chapbook from Hamilton the poet who wore a picture of a pig named "Hammy" on his shirt. I asked him to sign it.

"Hey, that poem was solid. Do you have a book out yet?" Hamilton asked, signing my chapbook in blue ink.

"Not yet," I replied.

"Well, I think your time is coming soon. Keep writing, Miss Traci."

If a guy wearing a shirt that says "Hammy" can self-publish and get ten bucks a pop for his thoughts, I realized I could surely do the same thing.

Traci Ann

Parallel Synchronicity
09.9.14

Todd Matthews and I have led parallel lives since 2009. We travel, create, volunteer, and work separately, but we have always been on matching wavelengths. We seem to always be in touch when something monumental is taking place in our lives.

Todd and I met in New Orleans in 2009. I was his construction site leader during his time volunteering in the rebuild effort post Hurricane Katrina. I showed him how to tile a bathroom, operate a nail gun, and mud drywall. We spent that Halloween running around the French quarter highly intoxicated on Jameson; I was dressed fittingly as a construction worker with a yellow hard hat, and he wielded a cap gun in a plastic holster on his cowboy costume.

Another time, in 2012, after my trip backpacking through Central and South America, he almost convinced me to jump on a sailboat out of Ft. Lauderdale that he was sailing to Mexico on with some friends.

This monumental moment wasn't about a sailboat or rebuilding homes. It was about keeping my job identity as an outdoor educator. Most recently, Todd has been working as a wilderness therapy guide in Utah. I had meant to touch base with him and ask about his experience working in wilderness therapy. I wanted to ask him for advice, and the mid-afternoon quiet in Heather's apartment presented a great time to reach out. I grabbed my phone and texted him while I pet Cody on the futon.

Traci: *Hey, are you around? If so, can we talk wilderness therapy a little? I just resigned from my outdoor job in New Orleans and I am driving west soon, heading to New Mexico.*

I put the phone down and listened to Cody's purring. Todd's text came back fast.

Todd: *Hey! Yes. I've got just the thing for you. I am leaving for Costa Rica in twelve hours. Call me.*

Of course he is leaving for Costa Rica in twelve hours. Probably off to change the world again. I would expect nothing less than this from Todd.

I called. He answered on the second ring. "Hey Trace!" He sounded excited.

"Hey bud, how are ya?"

"I'm great! Can't believe I'm leaving, in, like, twelve hours." There was a lot of background noise; he was clearly out and about somewhere. "Dude, Traci, drive one more state past New Mexico—to Utah! There is world-class skiing, mountaineering, canyoneering, and camping. The best part is no one is here because everyone thinks Utah is only for Mormons. It's like the Central America of the US!" He delivered his Utah pitch enthusiastically.

Todd works for a wilderness therapy company called Compass of Hope, based out of this mysterious Mormon land. "Trace, you would be perfect for this job, you have the soft skills, the big heart—don't worry about how to ski or the canyoneering, they pay to have you professionally trained." Todd's passion was contagious. "The kids are amazing and it's incredible to watch them grow during a backcountry trip."

"Wow, this sounds awesome," I said, stoked and fully committed to the magic he spoke over the phone. "But wait, if this gig is so great, why are you going to Costa Rica in twelve hours?" I asked.

"It's for Compass of Hope! They added a therapeutic program in Costa Rica. I'm being flown down to help setup the new training facility. Isn't that crazy?" He was out of breath.

"Are you okay?" I asked, the background noises still prevalent.

"Yeah, sorry, I'm racing around the Salt Lake Target buying some last minute toiletries for this trip," he answered.

"Todd that is amazing! I want a company I can grow in with good people. I didn't have that in New Orleans."

"Trace, seriously, send a resume and application soon. Mention my name in the cover letter. Text me once you do, and I will call the staffing coordinator. We're tight; I'll tell him what a great field guide you are," he said affirmatively.

"But what about my car? Where do I live? And with who?" I started to spiral.

"Traci, you know better than anyone how to follow your instinct and be brave. I came out here last year feeling very similar. I had everything in my car, and wanted to make a difference using the outdoors." I could hear the bleep of the Target scanner at the checkout counter. "The most beautiful part about all of it was, once I got out here I realized that thirty of the most authentic human beings just happened to have had the same idea—and they are all in Utah, working for this company." He laughed at the end. I could tell he was smiling.

"I think I will have time to fire off a resume once I get to Austin." I was excited.

"Great. You are amazing and you deserve an amazing place to work! I have to go, though—can't believe they are sending me to Costa Rica!"

"Thank you, Todd. So good to talk to you buddy." I missed him, my globe-trotting friend.

"Anytime Trace, good luck."

I hung up the phone and did a little happy dance in the apartment. Stella watched, wagging her tail with curiosity.

Did I really just get a job referral to a multi-million-dollar wilderness therapy company in Utah from one of the head field guides who I just happened to have taught how to tile a bathroom four years ago in the lower ninth ward?

Yep. That just happened. Ask and it shall be given. Yes. That's me. The badass-adventure-guide-writer-queen. Hell yes, universe.

One point for the westward team.

TRACI ANN

How to Remember 9/11
09.11.14

September 11th. The day when some assholes from across the world nailed my home state with hatred in the form of fiery airplanes. It has been thirteen years and CNN still thinks the best way to commemorate and honor deceased New Yorkers is to replay the video footage of the second plane careening into the other twin tower. It is so fucked up. They play it like an NFL referee plays back a Superbowl play; it's overly dramatized and in poor taste to watch on repeat in agonizing slow motion.

As Americans, we also seem to commemorate tragedy by reminding each other where we were on this earth when said tragedy happened. I was sitting in tenth grade study hall, cramming for a seventh-period Biology test. Heather was learning how to sing in her high school choir class.

I, too, lost loved ones during 9/11. Yes, CNN, we know it was intense. 9/11 will always be an intense day of history.

Personally, 9/11 will now be intense for a new reason: I purchased a camping stove at REI and finished a 5k during my final day in Atlanta.

I waltzed out of downtown Atlanta's REI not thinking about airplanes crashing into things they were not supposed to. I thought about how good it is going to feel cooking a pot of rice and beans on my new Pocket Rocket backpacking stove. In my head, this camp stove's debut will be in Big Bend National Park as my random journey heads into the depths of western Texas. I also bought a shiny four-piece aluminum cookware set, one red canister of propane fuel, and three freeze-dried bags of dinner entrees. This purchase completed the final room of my car home-the kitchen.

"Well, well, looks like somebody's going camping!" The cashier said. His little nametag said Paul.

"Yep!" I beamed, dumping the contents of my new kitchen onto the checkout counter.

"Where you taking this fancy little stove?" Paul asked. "Good choice by the way, this one's got a lot of pep to it," he added.

"Big Bend, headed to Austin first to see a friend," I said.

"Ah! What a gorgeous place. You got a week off a work or what?" Paul was a curious REI cashier, probably about forty-five, with a reddish beard.

"Nah, I'm on a road trip. Heading west through Texas for a while," I said, not sure how much Paul really wanted to know about me and my new kitchen.

"Boy, what I wouldn't give to have freedom like that!"

Would you give up the whole previous concept of yourself and shove your life into a car to get to Big Bend, Paul?

"Well you enjoy, young lady," he said, handing me my receipt and bag of kitchen.

When I put the REI purchases in the trunk a burly black man walked by and took an extra-long look in my trunk. "Looks like you live in there sweetheart!" He said laughing out loud to himself.

"It seems to be the case, eh?" I joined in his laughter, overtaken by how comical it truly was. I do live in there. He continued on his way through the baking-hot parking lot.

I stood back for a minute and admired my home. Two dressers, in the form of an Osprey sixty-liter pack and a beat-up brown suitcase, occupied the center of the trunk, both filled with clothing. The bedroom hid behind the clothing; a ten-degree down sleeping bag, two-person tent, inflatable Thermarest, plaid camp pillow, and a homemade survival kit. In the front of the trunk was now the kitchen, my new prized stove and all of its glorious accessories. A mini Walgreens also sat privately behind the driver's side chair, the three tiered white plastic container I had so deftly squeezed into the Chevy. It was equipped with soaps, toothbrushes, and medicines I can sell off the street if this trip turns sideways.

Well then, I really do live in my car right now. Life is so unpredictable. I love you, life; I hate you, life. Why do other people get to live in big amazing homes?

Because they are drinking the Kool-Aid. If following your truth was easy, I'm sure I'd have encountered more folks with their entire life inside of their sedans by now.

The evening 9/11 commemoration event was really wet, sticky, and aromatic. Heather took me back to Peachtree Running Club for the Thursday night adventure run. Now, as was the case last week I only made it one and a half miles in and had to wave the white flag. Tonight was different. We ran slower, I breathed deeper and I almost finished. We ran 2.9 miles before I needed to stop, lest I drown in a pool of my own sweat. Even though we were the last two people back to the storefront, we were greeted with Gatorade, clapping, and smiles. My body was electrified with accomplishment and smelled ripe.

"Bit by bit," Heather said high-fiving me.

"Bit by bit," I echoed back in between swigs of yellow Gatorade.

For me, this year's 9/11 was all about moving forward, pressing into my personal limits, and buying a tiny stove I can cook outside with. That was so much better than watching the twin towers fall over and over again.

Things fall apart, for sure, but there is beauty in the breakdown. I think of the freedom tower that shines bright these days in that epic skyline of steel beams and city lights. Just like the freedom tower, all 5'2" of me stands tall in my uncertain world.

Holding a brand new camping stove.

TRACI ANN

Lessons from Couchsurfers in Lafayette

09.12.14

It was still dark when I left Heather's apartment.

"Be careful, and take care of yourself," she said, wiping the fog from her glasses.

"I will, thanks so much for all of this. You're such a good friend." We hugged quickly outside my car.

"Good luck out west, you'll find what you need to find, I'm sure of it," she said, and yawned.

I bombed past downtown Atlanta, taking in the cityscape once more. My next destination is Austin. Since that is rather far from Atlanta I decided to stay one night in Lafayette, Louisiana, a place I have always wanted to visit during my tenure as a Louisiana resident, but never made the effort. Today I would chase the sunrise west; traveling back the way I had come on the interstates and through New Orleans to Lafayette, where a couchsurfer had agreed to host me for a night.

I stopped in Montgomery for breakfast around 9 a.m. and ate a Chik-Fil-A biscuit sandwich. I had already passed the spot on I-85 where the deadly accident had occurred a week earlier. Even though I traveled on the unlucky side of the interstate, I was still spared and given my flavorful chicken breakfast.

At mid-day I was not prepared for the reaction my body and energy field had when I began to see signs for New Orleans. A mundane morning on the road morphed into an internal firestorm of emotions. I crossed the state line and felt a sharp pain in my stomach; hot anger circulated through my body. I replayed that Monday morning in Steph's office, a weekend removed from my somber resignation.

We stood facing each other, both wearing our familiar orange work T-shirts, both with our mousey brown hair pulled back into low ponytails. Her eyes were heavy with concern, yet weirdly ambivalent. Steph had called me into her office after I had put away the canoe paddles from a morning lesson on the bayou. She told me to shut the door. Her office door was only shut when she was either on the phone with her wife or scheduling a program with a school. I didn't like the door being shut.

"Look, in light of your resignation last week, I don't think you should attend the staff meeting we have scheduled for tomorrow." She crossed her arms over her chest, and looked down at her feet.

I was shocked. "Why not? Don't you want me to let the guys know I only have two weeks of work left?" I tried to stand tall, but my voice sounded like a wounded soldier.

"Look Trace, we are moving forward with program-related goals, staff goals..." Her voice trailed off for a moment. "If you tell everyone why you are leaving, I am concerned it will make your last two weeks with us very draining."

The manipulation was palpable. She was banning me from work to buy herself a bit of time to cover her ass. That moment was like a knife to the stomach, a knife we used to do fish-filet demonstrations. It is so sharp in its intention, one barely needs to exert force, just precision.

"Stephanie, I want to tell them why, in overarching terms, that I am leaving work. That this environment no longer suits me." I puffed out my chest a little to appear bigger.

She stared at me blankly, hiding the hurt for a later date. "Traci, I don't know what you want from me," she huffed, slightly agitated that I hadn't already left her office.

"What I want is to know that what just happened to me—being sexually harassed—will not happen again on your watch. I want you to take steps to help fix this problem!" I pointed harshly at the floor with my index finger. "You can't ban me from coming to work. What you're doing is illegal!" I snapped.

"I think you need to leave my office." She opened the door and pointed to the hallway.

"Fine," I replied, and left for the day.

That was the last time I saw Steph.

I decided I would use my day off now for one thing—to write out a full complaint to human resources, and nail NORP's fucked-up ass to the wall in Baton Rouge.

I walked aimlessly around the Louisiana welcome center in the mid-day downpour, trying to wash off that horrible memory. I went inside and cried in a bathroom stall for a solid fifteen minutes. I left the welcome center clutching my free coffee and map of Lafayette sniffling sadly. I wondered if the pain would ever go away.

Would I ever miss New Orleans the way I used to? Or would it now forever represent a place that I was drastically mistreated by people I held close?

I passed the Superdome as fast as I could, focusing on getting to Lafayette safely and not sobbing the whole ride there.

I love the couchsurfing community. Couchsurfing is a global network of folks who graciously put up their couches for wayfaring travelers to sleep on for free. The goal of couchsurfing is to connect like-minded people so they can share meals, conversation, and couches. I have "surfed" all over the world in my travels and slept on all sorts of surfaces, so I was excited to do it once again in Lafayette.

This couchsurfing experience was exactly what my soul needed. It was nearing dinnertime when the Chevy and I finally arrived to Lafayette. We had navigated intermittent torrential rain all the way from the state line. I pulled into Wendi's driveway and noticed I was inside of a cul-de-sac with immaculate homes. Wendi's home was stunning from the outside; floor-to-ceiling windows and a freshly cut, deep green lawn. This was my first time seeking out a member older than I was. Normally I opted to stay at places that were close to the action of the city I was visiting. Since, however, this was just a layover before Austin, I didn't mind her house being out in the suburbs a bit.

Wendi's profile on the couchsurfing website is what spurred me to send a request. It said she was a two-time breast cancer survivor who liked to live gratefully and run ultra-marathons. I was attracted to her bright smile on her profile as she posed with her friends after a marathon race.

Wendi opened the front door on the first doorbell ring. She was tall, extremely thin, and her smile looked just as warm in person as the photo.

"Traci! Come in!" She hugged me immediately. I collapsed slightly into her hug, feeling the weight of my emotions. Without knowing it, Wendi held me in my hurt, madness, and exhaustion.

"Put your bag down, you must be tired! All the way from Atlanta…do you want some tea?" She escorted me into her enormous kitchen where another woman, slightly older, was already sitting.

"Yes, I would love some tea." I replied.

The older slender woman looked up happily from her steaming mug of tea and got off the kitchen barstool to hug me as well. "You must be Traci! I am Susan, also a couchsurfer. Wendi agreed to host me last minute as well. I hear you are a writer. So am I!" Her academic tone gave her away. "So happy you are here." Susan's sweet disposition mellowed any residual sadness that I had been carrying from my earlier transit through New Orleans.

The rest of the evening was a whirlwind of good vibes and conversation from uplifting women. Immediately Wendi talked openly of her struggle with breast cancer and how it forced her down a transformative path of constant gratitude. Susan spoke of the gift economy and how she has been traveling around the US staying at people's homes in exchange for doing minor housekeeping and gardening. Her eyes were bright, filled with hope and love.

We finished our tea and Wendi treated all of us to dinner at an Italian restaurant. I feasted on a seafood pasta in a cream sauce and marveled at the amazing women the universe had sent to me.

"I believe there is no time to waste in doing the things that you love and doing everything in the name of happiness," Wendi said with gusto, after a big bite of her chicken parm. I raised my glass.

"To chasing happiness and being kind," I said. We toasted our wine glasses.

The whole evening was a blur of magic. Both women, so much older, filled with so many additional life experiences charged me up through my bones. I laid awake for a while in Wendi's guestroom, indulging in the soft queen bed with too many pillows. I tried to rewind and capture all of the wisdom Susan and Wendi had given to me in five short waking hours.

I rolled over in the fluffy bed and clicked on the bedroom lamp, then searched in my backpack for my journal and pen. I didn't want to forget the profound and funny tidbits of wisdom these two well-traveled ladies had shared with me.

Lessons from Couchsurfers in Lafayette:

Don't talk too much about yourself, there is way too much to learn from others and never enough time to hear every story.

Be open to the journey and you will receive a bed as soft as your wildest dreams in a gorgeous home with the kindest people.

Fear is truly the only thing holding any of us back.

Hug on arrival, even if you have never met.

Go deep on the conversations topics right away; spirit, gift economy—cut the bullshit—what squares your moon, baby? I don't give a damn about what you do during the hours of nine to five.

Three generations of women at a dinner table sharing their story is mind boggling and humbling.

Walk bravely into the dark and know the universe will turn the light on, one lovely bulb at a time. Admire each illumination equally.

Practice fierce gratitude and it will return to you tenfold.

Don't dance excessively during the '70s in bad shoes, or you will not be able to drive a stick shift, let alone walk very well. That is, if you have the ability to teleport to the '70s and dance excessively.

Listen, and hold space for the collective story.

When faced with death, look it directly in the eye and say, "What else you got for me?"

Drink fancy tea and wear amazing socks—life is too short to do otherwise.

Be love, send love, show up.

TRACI ANN

Part Three: Austin

Strip away the fear, underneath, it's all the same love.
- Macklemore

TRACI ANN

Sharing Meals
09.14.14

I made it to Austin. So far, so delicious.

When I jumped in my car two weeks ago I never expected to eat so well on this trip. I just figured eating ramen or leftovers on the way to each place would be par for the course. As the theme of this trip would dictate, the universe whispered, "lean in," and I did. I leaned right into some southern hospitality and good home cooking.

Christina opened the door to her hip, red, solar powered home, and I was tackled with the smell of roasted chicken and a bear hug.

"Oh my God, I haven't seen you in forever!" Christina squealed, holding me by the shoulders in her doorway. She pulled me in for a second hug and I felt how petite we both were—our bodies fit together like puzzle pieces.

Christina is another friend I met while teaching the ways of rebuilding homes. She volunteered the same year Todd Matthews did. She loved cutting the ceramic tiles on the wet saw for a floor we were installing. I have many amazing friends, but not many can hold a candle to Christina. By day she wears the most stylish outfits and works at a smart tech startup, by night she's been known to dance in burlesque shows, wearing very stylish nothingness. She and I have been friends ever since her volunteer stint; held together by a shared love for Saints football and great books, we have maintained a distance friendship for years. I messaged her the details of life and my plan to travel through Texas a few weeks back. She offered her guestroom in Austin and insisted I stop by to stay with her. I obliged graciously.

"Tell me everything! How was Atlanta?" Christina asked as she opened the oven to check on the herb roasted chicken. I arrived just in time to attend a dinner party she was throwing for me, her boyfriend, and four other close friends.

"Atlanta was wonderful. Heather was so good to me. We cooked so many dinners together, went on runs, and I took her to see some tiny houses in a parking garage," I giggled at the end, thinking of the tiny home adventure.

"So, how are you doing with leaving NOLA? Any word on what human resources is going to do about all the shit you reported?" Christina pulled out a cutting board and began chopping purple cabbage.

"Nothing yet," I replied, studying the colorful tattoo on her arm.

"I still can't believe all of that happened to you..." Christina paused her chopping and looked at me empathetically.

"They said they will conduct a formal investigation and talk to each person I named confidentially. It was supposed to happen this week, actually." I looked at my feet and then back at her.

"Stay positive girl. You are so brave for standing up like that. I've always admired the way you walk so powerfully to the beat of your own drum." Christina stood on her tip-toes and snatched a stack of plates from the cabinet above her head. I admired her ass in her jeans for just a second.

She handed me half the stack of pastel-colored plates. I began to place the plates around the table when it hit me. Home-cooked food. Steph. Sharing meals. I miss sharing meals with my boss-roommate Steph.

Fuck. I drifted back to that cold and gloomy December afternoon last year.

"You can live with me for three weeks while you look for a new rental, and then you will find a place and it'll all work. You are a valuable member of the staff and I want to support you," Steph said, grasping a mug of café au lait, sitting relaxed in her chair at the café in City Park.

We arranged the meeting after a blustery day of winter

programming to talk about where I stood with work. My lease lapsed on a rental that I could no longer afford in the rapidly gentrifying neighborhoods of New Orleans. I loved my work. I hated that I was being bullied and harassed by my co-workers. There was nowhere remotely affordable to live and continue working in the outdoors full-time.

"It is truly up to you, but I do have an extra bedroom in my house. You could pay what you can afford, and help me with the dog," Steph continued, dumping another creamer into her mug. I gazed out the window, hoping the correct answer was written in the clouds.

Live with my gay boss, why not? What could possibly go wrong? I had a fifty-fifty shot of it working. I also had nowhere to live except in my newly purchased five by ten storage unit with its orange metal door.

"Are you sure it's okay?" I asked.

"Yeah, who knows, we might even become friends," she replied, her tone optimistic.

"I would love to do that, Steph. We could do the three weeks and go from there," I said, relieved and excited to know my boss in a whole new way.

I ended up living with my boss-roommate for six months. That was a lot of time to share meals and get to know a sister. We walked her long-haired wiener dog on the bayou at dusk, drank margaritas every Wednesday night, and cooked meals together on Sundays. Every Monday her mother and father came over for red beans and rice. They would hug me goodbye and say, "I love you."

I was like the younger sister.

When the spring came, we went running so she could get in shape for her June wedding. We left work at work, and joked about how I had the ability to laugh at the stupidest shit. We got drunk at Jazzfest and ate disgusting amounts of fried festival food.

I really enjoyed living at my boss-roommate's house. After most meals we found ourselves outside on the porch, under the increasingly humid night sky. We would drink white wine and bullshit about life. My heart swelled with gratitude for finding a home of love and mutual respect.

Remember the fifty-fifty odds? Fifty-fifty gets fucked when you throw in other variables like being bullied at work on the daily and constantly hearing sly comments about how good I was looking in my red mini skirt. I am not a gambling lady, but when you end up in a setup where the hand that cuts your paycheck also fluffs your pillows, well then you are just all in, baby.

I lived with my boss-roommate for six fun, weird, eye-opening months. I went all in at the end—divulging the full story of the harassment, while simultaneously agreeing to write a blessing for Steph's wedding. That's when the odds went in the dealer's favor.

How can your whole world crumble and flip so fast? Why does losing friends hurt like scraped knees, and when does the stinging stop?

Now I find myself in Austin, abruptly without my boss-roommate friendship. It blew up like a Molotov cocktail in my eyeballs. Steph never hugged me before I left. The last meal we shared was at a taqueria on her birthday in August, two days before I resigned. I bought us pork tamales and margaritas.

There will always be loss. You usually can't see it because it is hiding behind what you will win. I lost a boss-roommate-friend-temporary sister. I did, however, gain self-respect, a spontaneous road trip, and many kind souls who also like to share meals.

The door to Christina's solar home swung open and two young couples and her boyfriend, Kevin, walked into the house. Christina squealed in happiness again and ran over to hug everyone who had arrived, saving a kiss for her attractive man.

"Guys this is my friend Traci from New Orleans! She is on a road trip heading to New Mexico," Christina said, pointing both her hands at me, presenting me like an item at show and tell. I shook everyone's hand

and we all sat down to an amazing spread: golden-brown chicken, brussel sprouts roasted in olive oil and garlic, a cabbage dish with Sriracha sauce, and cornbread with a honey glaze.

"That is so cool you are just traveling around like that!" Julia said from across the table. She was Jared's girlfriend. "I went to Burning Man a few weeks back and it was incredible." She wore a plaid shirt over a whimsical yellow tank top, cropped jean shorts, and brown heeled boots. She was the poster child of hipsters everywhere, and I loved it.

"Yeah, I am headed to Big Bend next week to solo camp for my first time, pretty excited," I said and savored the rich taste of the cornbread.

"Oh man, I went camping there in June. You will love it. It is amazing, and so far removed from everything. Make sure you bring extra water and stuff," Jared advised, glancing around the table for the bowl of cabbage salad. Jared looked like an outdoorsy guy, with a big red beard and muscles that pulled his waffle shirt tight.

"Christina. This food is so delicious," Kevin announced, grabbing her small hand across the table. He raised his glass of champagne towards the center of the table and we all followed his lead. "To sharing a meal with great people," he said, the cement floor amplifying his statement. Glassware clinked together and the room was filled with animated stories, love, and people sharing a meal.

Hot Wax and Self Doubt
09.15.14

Today had a similar tempo to a week ago in Atlanta when I went out on that solo day hike. I relished in sleeping in Christina's comfy guest bed, made French press coffee ever so delicately and crafted a breakfast of bagels, eggs, and chicken sausage. I browsed the internet on the subject of my new passion, the tiny home. Early on, self-doubt started to whisper tattered nothings into my ear.

"This is foolish, you will never build your own home." Its voice was raspy. "Why do you keep traveling west with no plans?"

Shut up. Shut up. Shut up.

I paced around Christina's kitchen, engulfed in self-criticism—a habit I need to break, but don't totally know how yet. Mental chatter, when you are on the bottom of the bell curve of transitional grief, is gritty. It pushes you so hard into your own being you can actually feel your skin stretching just a tad further than you would like. You are stretching and evolving into a newer version of yourself, though it is hard to see just yet.

Change and self-doubt feel akin to a great eyebrow waxing. You sign the waiver that hopefully you are not allergic to pine resin and lay down in the chair, a chaotic mess of unkempt brows. The stylist, hopefully not named Betty, stretches your skin, applies hot wax then the pristine canvas strip. She rubs the area, making sure the wax has adhered. Doubt arises. *Maybe this isn't such a good idea, this will hurt, and I don't really need sexy eyebrows...*

Too late. Hot pain sears, branding your skin. She hands you the mirror, your flesh still tingling, stimulated from all the pulling of hair by their roots. You look in the mirror and well, damn girl, you be looking fine. Change is painful; she takes away old pieces of you and makes room for the new parts.

I calmed my ego just enough to taste my chicken sausage and plan the rest of my time in Austin. I wanted to attend another poetry reading, swim at Barton Springs, do some yoga, and check out some more alternative housing projects. Christina had mentioned that Mobile Loaves and Fishes non-profit were in the midst of creating a new sustainable community for the homeless just outside the city limits. I finished my chicken sausage and dialed their number.

"Mobile Loaves and Fishes, this is Gina, how can I help you?" a tender voice on the line said.

"Yes, hi, I am traveling through Austin and heard about the sustainable community y'all are building with and for the homeless. I am very interested in smaller, sustainable houses. I was wondering if you offer tours to the public?" I replied.

"Why yes, we do. Always looking to educate more people about how to live in collective community! Do you happen to be around this afternoon?" Gina's tone was genuine and loving.

"Yep, I am!" I said back, trying to match her upbeat tone.

"Come out in two hours and ask for me at the first trailer you see, I will show you around and answer any questions you have."

I finished my coffee, got dressed for the day, and tossed self-doubt out the window as I drove away from the Austin skyline towards another unplanned adventure.

The tour was great. Gina was a heavier set lady with short blonde hair. She drove up to me in a golf cart and we rode all around the property; I was stoked to see a value menu in the making of sustainable housing such as retrofitted air streams, small cottages, elevated tents, and a community garden. I thought of my future hippie commune and my soul began to fill up with self-confidence again.

This is not foolish. I can build my own home, and I will.

You Fancy the Women Folk?

09.16.14

Shiiiiit.

I noticed the clumps of mud and dirt that had accumulated on the bottom of Christina's designer gray and white guest room towel. I had taken it on the adventure to Barton Springs, a natural spring fed swimming hole within the Austin city limits. I didn't think twice about bringing her towel because I didn't have my own.

Christina has such fancy things. She is so cool. My mind fluttered around.

I got her designer towel even more dirty with my traveling life; unable to turn back now as my bathing suit was soaked from a refreshing plunge of sixty-eight-degree water and my bare feet deposited more wet grass on the towel.

Damn that girl is so chill; nice house, sexy, she makes me laugh so hard.

Maybe it was the sun. The heat of Texas. The delirium of traveling west in exile mode. I decided to entertain the idea of women folk again.

What would it be like to date a lady?

My first year living in New Orleans, I rocked a hardcore stereotypical lesbian fauxhawk haircut and worked construction. That year I received a puzzling amount of lady date offers as I wielded a hammer, tool belt and spikey hair. Most offers I met with a look of bewilderment. Other times, my aloof disposition made it appear like a chase. I did end up on a lady date in New Orleans once.

"Based on *that* message, that girl is asking you on a date," Matt, my boyfriend at the time, said pointing to my computer screen.

"No it's not! She just wants to meet new friends," I replied innocently, naïve to my twenty-four-year-old world.

"*Mhmm*," Matt said, pursing his big lips and raising an eyebrow. "Well, text me when you realize it's a date and I will come get ya. I will be up the street having drinks with the guys," he said. He kissed me and walked out of the house, laughing to himself.

Looking back on the meet up with this girl, I have no idea where my rational mind was. All signs pointed to the fact that I was indeed on my first girl date. She ordered us a large cocktail to sip from together, positioning it in the middle of the table. She told me I was adorable and fawned over my sweet brown eyes. I'm not gonna lie, I like to receive compliments, so we sat in the tavern booth eating burgers, and I smiled coyly as she complimented me again and again. The night went on and I started yawning all over the booth—not out of boredom, but because I was so tired from those summer days of nailing siding to homes.

"Looks like I need to take you home there sleeping beauty—or to my place," she said gruffly, her tone masculine. She was ready to take charge of me. Her words rustled me awake.

Eeep! I am on a girl date! She is trying to take me home with her; what am I going to do?!

"I need to use the restroom," I said, excusing myself, darting into the single bathroom. I pulled my cell from my purse and called up Matt. "I'm on a girl date," I said sheepishly.

He laughed for a good while. "What gave you that impression? She wanna know what's in your tool belt?" He couldn't handle how funny he was. I wanted to wring his neck.

"Matt! She wants to drive me home in her pick-up truck. *Matt*, come get me!" I pleaded, horribly embarrassed, wondering why he let me act like a fool.

"Okay, I will be there in five, I am two bars up the road," he said.

I scooted back into the booth and prayed Matt would make it on time.

"You okay there, lady?" my date said, laying her credit card down on the check. I nodded, suddenly feeling very vulnerable. The server returned with the charged bill and she signed it quickly.

"Well then, let's get out of here, get your tired self all ready for bed." She bit her lower lip. The jig was up. I didn't know what to do. Comical fright spread through my reality—where was Matt? Moments later a tall black silhouette registered in my periphery. I turned to my right, meeting Matt's lips with mine as he shoved himself into the booth next to me.

"Hi, I'm Matt, Traci's boyfriend," he said, extending a muscular arm to my lady date. She shook his hand in confusion, introducing herself back.

The next ten minutes were the most awkward of my life. The three of us tried to small talk; about the Saints improving record, about drill bits, manly things. Matt and my lady tried to one-up each other on macho things before I interjected to stop the bizarre madness I had so willingly agreed to in the first place.

"Alright Matt, I am really tired. Bring me home please?" I asked, kicking him under the table.

"Alright," he replied. We waved goodbye to her on the sidewalk, Matt's hand around my waist.

"Well, maybe next time you can ride home on my motorcycle," she said brazenly. Matt and I stood in the dark sidewalk, wide-eyed.

"Dude, she wanted you so bad," he said, all out of laughter for the night.

"Yeah...weird," I said, jumping in the front of his black truck.

My first lady date was a disaster; foolish, awkward, and I didn't even know I was on one to truly evaluate it. I buried any new feelings that registered that night and continued to date Matt.

Today, I unearthed the girl feelings at Barton Springs. Swished the ideas around like mouthwash. I swallowed all of it, pride and future ill-placed shame included. Austin is a weird city—it makes you feel like you can do anything, including entertain your new self-concept that is being sculpted before your eyes. I laid on Christina's fancy towel on the sloped grass overlooking the city skyline and contemplated being with a woman. On different terms. On my own, informed terms.

Last night, as we shared a gorgeous spread of vegan food at a quaint local spot, Christina told me she had dated women exclusively for ten years until very recently. When did I miss this boat? She's so put together as a straight woman—with her handsome, steady boyfriend, talking of disposable income and kitchenware. When did she kiss women and what did it look like? What did it feel like, as another woman, to be wrapped up with her? Who balanced the male and female energy, or is that just the analytical oversight of a beginner?

Who knows. I kept thinking about it all day. Obviously as of late the male sex has disappointed me in their caliber of humanity. They seem to think their two balls and flaccid penis have a mind of their own, which should be taken very seriously…even forcefully. Sorry guys, but lately, I am not impressed by the cock. By men. By men who talk about my pussy behind my back. By men who fantasize about leaving their wife to ravish me in the sack, and then blame it on pent-up frustration that they can only vocalize through scandalous text messages at night.

I am however, impressed by two things: how many raging hot lesbian couples there are in Austin and how turned on I get by watching *Orange is the New Black* on Netflix.

After a quick nap back at Christina's, post womenfolk meditation at Barton Springs, I continued the exercise of free spiritedness by watching the second episode of this hot drama about an all-women's prison. Alex and Piper were complicated lovers outside of prison and then found themselves inside the same pen for a crime they had committed together a decade earlier. Even in prison, the scenes of the two main actresses kissing up against a brick wall caused me to flinch and double take in delight. My nipples hardened under my shirt. Maybe I would like a woman to finger me? God knows it takes a really skilled man to figure out how to spin the tracks on my clitoris just right. Perhaps women just do all of the sexy times stuff better because they know how to be touched. However, they lack that critical stiff penis that enters on intercourse with such power.

Perhaps…both? Yes, yes that's what I want. Sexy times with both genders. Both penis and vagina, on separate occasions.

My final delve into womenfolk-related sexy times was observing the droves of incredibly hot lady couples who were at the Austin slam poetry night. Before the slam began I watched in awe as female couple after couple walked, hand in hand into the old-school theater. They wore lipstick and cute dresses, some had tattoos, and others had more masculine clothing on. They all acted like hetero couples do; sneaking a quick peck on the lips in between poets, leaning into each other to feel the warmth and magnetism of body against body.

The poetry was incredible; the artists were so talented and they all spoke their truth so hard I got a lady boner. Poet after poet, trigger warning after trigger warning, I snuck glimpses of lady couples and tried to picture myself in such a relationship. Would it work? Which energy would I bring? Would I miss the feeling of a hard dick entering me? Is it wrong to feel attracted to both?

Clearly this is a part of my life that needs to be explored more and nurtured in love and not shame. Thankfully a pristine oasis of desert called Big Bend waits in the near future, where I can potentially decide if I want to let bi-curiosity kill the cat.

TRACI ANN

No Second Chances
09.17.14

Today was one of those obligatory prep, pack, plan days that a traveler must do in order to continue the journey forward. I don't love these days, but I don't hate them either. Just when I get settled in, enjoying a place, such as Christina's swanky home, I need to move on. I am staying in Austin another few days at a hostel, as her boyfriend's birthday is tonight. I took the hint and booked up the road.

After Austin, and after a short-yet-hopefully-magical day visiting and staying in a tiny home this Saturday in Luling Texas, it is on to Big Bend.

I'm traveling to Big Bend to camp and hike the trails for four full days. A solo camping endeavor. I thought feeling terrified to speak up about sexual harassment was the highest level of terror. So far, each subsequent piece of this impromptu car adventure has pushed me further and further out of my comfort zone.

Resign > file complaint > drive my car away from home > read poetry aloud > seriously contemplate bi-sexuality > camp alone in Big Bend National Park.

I took the new camp stove out of its pristine box. I set the triangular red box on Christina's kitchen table, marveling at it. I started to read the instructions on how to set it up, but quickly felt overwhelmed. I was afraid to use my virgin shiny Pocket Rocket camp stove that I just bought in the Atlanta REI. Absolutely petrified. Another new thing to learn: more self-sufficiency, fiercer living.

Keep going, an unknown magical voice gently said into my ear, convincing me to pick up the instruction pamphlet once more.

In a week from today I will have camped, hiked, and crossed the border into Mexico in a national park devoted to preserving the Chihuahuan desert. *Holy shit! I am doing this.*

I made the grocery list of camp food to prove it—granola, Gatorade powder, gallons of water, etc. I felt like a mix of *Tomb Raider* and *Strawberry Shortcake*. Badass and yet still soft, not processed enough from this wild and weird adventure.

Reading about Big Bend is intense. There are mountain lions, brown bears, and these pig- looking animals pronounced with a Spanish accent. I have no idea how a desolate national park ended up on my radar. Perhaps a friend shouted it out on my Facebook wall? Honestly, I can't remember. What I do know is that the images of Big Bend that I Googled—pictures of the sun setting over dry, reddish rocks—convinced me I needed to drive my white Chevy far across Texas, very close to Mexico, and experience the Google image in person.

Why is every next step so scary? Once you have stepped out and the terrain emerges in front of you, the first moment is over. You turn around and the path, the path you were so certain would not show up, has, and you have walked very far. Tears drop from your eyes; you have made it, but much to your dismay, you can never walk backwards on the path. We never get second chances on first experiences.

Life is an endless parade of joyous and terrifying endeavors. The initial fear present on first experiences will never go away, because it is rooted in the fragile human mind. Maybe if we can balance the fear and action, then we can be even more present to each endeavor.

Press me into it then, life, but I can't guarantee I won't scream bloody murder. I most likely will. And feel foolish and cry like an embarrassed baby afterwards. But, dear life, please push me into myself even more through whatever this road trip is meant to be.

We never get second chances on first experiences. This is my first time resigning from a job. This is my first time, perhaps, truly learning what I am made of.

Watching Bats
09.18.14

Tonight was my first night on the other side of the Colorado River. I checked into the hostel in the mid-afternoon. I rolled out the white sheets I was given and made my bed on the top bunk. Not as glamorous as Christina's, but it would do.

6 p.m. rolled around and I was feeling fidgety. There was music belting out across the street from the hostel. It echoed through the common room like a gust of wind every time someone walked through the front door. Unable to concentrate, I closed my book and walked up to the front desk.

"What's going on outside with the music?" I asked.

"A food truck round-up," the front desk girl with hairy armpits said. "You should check it out now," she added, "before it gets too packed with people getting done with work."

My stomach rumbled. Decision made by the hostel girl with hairy armpits and high-wasted shorts with leggings. I tossed my wallet, cell phone, and a map of Austin into my purse and strode out the door towards the music.

Austin is known for its food truck culture. This is a definitive portion of one's Austin stay. I approached and saw a blissful lineup of colorful trucks and mini buses giving off all sorts of smells. A tin-plated truck offered homemade ice cream, a mini yellow and green school bus sold Mexican fare. I caught sight of a red, white, and blue truck toting lobster rolls and the northerner in me got all nostalgic. I bellied up to the seafood truck and a handsome guy in a white and red polo greeted me.

"Hey there, what can I get for you?" he asked. His smile was so perfect, so charming. His blonde hair was neatly parted to one side.

"Yeah, can I please have one of the Connecticut-style rolls?" I asked, smiling back, excited to eat.

"Sure thing! Do you want scallions on top?"

"Yes," I replied.

He presented the lobster roll to me in a red-and-white checkered holder. I thanked him and found a spot in the grass to sit. The band was doing a sound check and the crowd was beginning to gather; people were setting up their lawn chairs and kids were being set free to roam the small contained grass area. The lobster was incredible; the Old Bay seasoning wafted into my nostrils strongly and the first bite was buttery seafood madness. I ate it with gusto. Then I tried to slow my noshing and savor each level of taste. It was too good. I noshed hard and the lobster disappeared all too quickly.

The band seemed a long way from starting their set, so I chucked my trash and made my way to the boardwalk over the river. My eyes traced the concrete path that wound up the left bank of the river, opposite the city skyline. I walked happily, belly full, watching others jog after their jobs, and walk their dogs in the disappearing sunlight.

Slowly a creeping sensation of unease started at my feet as tingles and moved towards my heart. I knew what it was; the ego cracking its whip of judgment. No job. Eating lobster rolls. Laughing at the employed folks and laughing even harder at the mounting traffic above the boardwalk on the interstate. My ego scolded such arrogant thinking with uncomfortable tingles.

I don't have a job. Shit. What does that mean?

Rather than grapple with myself again, I took a deep breath and called my soul-sister, Kelly. Kelly and I met two years ago in a hostel in Buenos Aires. We have only spent eight full days around each other—one day in Buenos Aires at a Starbucks and the other seven this past Mardi Gras when I fled to her hometown of Santa Cruz. We maintain a deep phone friendship, and agree on most things like the importance of following your heart, doing yoga, and eating free samples at all groceries stores whenever possible. This girl knows how to live life, and I love her for it. I knew she would be running around town at this time in California.

"Kelly! Girl, I'm on a nature boardwalk in Austin, heading to go see North America's largest colony of bats. Life is so random, right?" I stopped on the boardwalk to look at the sunset. I bullshitted with her a little more, talking about how oddly amazingly Austin was. My fidgeting returned.

"But Traci, how are *you* doing? Like, your spirit?" Kelly interrupted.

"Well, I'm okay," I paused to watch a young couple jog past me with a baby carriage. The tingles swirled up my legs. "Actually, I am not okay, Kel. I don't have a job, I'm just wandering through Texas with all my shit packed in my car, and I don't know what the meaning of all this is," I said, the pressure of salt water pushing against my tear ducts.

"Traci, babe, we is good, sister. You are good. I just went to Whole Foods and the craziest thing happened—it was their grand opening and they had free food for everyone!" I could hear Kelly crunching between her words. She was always eating when I talked to her on the phone; that's why I call her Cookie Monster, with utmost affection. "And, get this: I got an hour of free parking because someone fed the parking meter extra! Isn't life amazing?" Kelly's words splashed over me like a hot shower, comforting and refreshing. I watched the fish jump on the dusky river, absorbing what she was saying.

"I mean, I definitely feel the same way, especially now, since I only got back from Portugal last week and I don't have a job, either," she said. I heard her say hello to someone.

"I just feel lame," I said.

"Do you think it is on purpose how things are right now? Like, you and me not having jobs or babies, or husbands, but some of our friends do? If we were all the same we wouldn't grow," she said, posing it as a question and a statement.

"Yeah I know, everything in divine order," I replied. We'd had this conversation a million times.

"Observing the lifestyles of our counterparts offers us resistance which we can use to grow!" she proclaimed.

I love Kelly. She munched on a cookie and exhaled blissfully, still clearly roaming the aisles of Whole Foods.

"You're right, I like that. I mean, maybe my job today is just to eat good food, and go hang out with a bunch of tourists who are lining up along the Congress Avenue Bridge to watch the largest urban bat colony have a party at dusk," I said, and laughed. The boardwalk had given way to a dirt trail and I could see a crowd gathering near the bridge in front of me.

"Exactly, sister," she replied.

"Right, I am watching bats tonight. I am good," I said.

She exhaled through her mouth again. "We are *so* good, mama, right? Don't you feel it? This is a moment you will never get back; standing in the dusk overlooking a silly crowd of bat-loving tourists in Austin on a road trip that won't ever happen again." Her words were so comforting and filled with wisdom beyond her twenty-nine years.

I inhaled deeply. "You're right Kel, thanks for reminding me," I said.

"You just gotta be in it, Trace. We are so lucky! Each day, right now, we can wake up and say 'What do I want to do today?' And then go do it. Yeah there is going to be self-judgment, but perhaps the work of the unemployed is that of inner work. An internship in inner growth!" She said with passion. I was so thankful Argentina had brought us together.

"I wish you were here with me watching the bats!" I said, chuckling at the funny offer.

"I am, mama. We are always near—if not in body, in spirit," she said.

We laughed hysterically for a while about how I was indeed watching bats materialize from underneath a dark bridge in Austin with the gorgeous cool blue twilight sky as the backdrop.

Watching bats in Austin. I am, just be. Just be, or perish in thought.

I watched the bats flutter around, listened to the tourists whisper *oohs* and *aahs*, and felt grateful to be unemployed, and free to roam about to as many bat gatherings as I wanted.

Fingered
09.19.14

It was a hot and sticky morning as I rolled around in the top bunk of my hostel bed. When I completed my full roll to the other side of the pillow I reached for my watch. 7 a.m. Light was peering through the red curtains, and I noticed the room smelled of feet. Gross. The AC broke last night, so I had to roll with the wet, hot, feet-smelling woes of a hosteller's plight.

One more night. No big deal. You have stayed in bamboo huts on remote islands, and cabins in Patagonia...this is nothing, Trace.

What happened next gave me the criteria needed to classify this stay as the weirdest hostel stay ever. The watch said 7 a.m. I had nothing to do, so I inhaled smelly feet and rolled back over to get some more damp sleep.

That's when it started. A mild thwacking sound, like water rapidly slapping against a dock. The eerily familiar sound was coming from the depths of the bunk below me and one whole metal bunk bed away. It was the sound of moist fingers flicking a clitoris. There were intermittent deep exhales and tiny moans.

Is this chick for real? When did she bring home a dude?

This girl had checked in after I left for my bat adventure last night, when did she have time to wrangle a fuck buddy? Then it occurred to me that, for every tiny moan, there was no matching male sound. He wasn't asking her, "Yeah, right there, babe?" as he pleasured her. He wasn't asking, because *he* was not there. Nobody was with her in the twin bed below.

I waited. I listened intently. I know that sounds weird, but I wanted to confirm what was actually going on: that the stinky Asian woman who had checked in last night with a conspicuous suitcase filled with bags of cheese puffs, Pringles, and chocolate, was indeed masturbating in an eight-woman dorm room.

I waited. Nothing. 7:10 a.m. The creepy hosteller starting thwacking away again at rapid speed. Like a DJ on a turntable trying to mix house beats with reggae.

Oh my God. Oh my fucking God.

A rage of anger ran through my mind. I paid the same amount to sleep here too—why does she think she can finger herself in a room occupied with eight other people? *Just because we are all women, that makes it okay?* I thrashed my sheets around, cleared my throat loudly, trying to make her stop. *I'm going to the front desk and demanding a refund!* Not only was I sexiled from East Austin, I was receiving a $26 lesbian morning delight if I chose to go down from my bunk.

Maybe if she didn't smell like feet. I was thoroughly disgusted. That's not the kind of woman-sexy-times I was after. I wanted hot, intelligent, feminine-woman action; not stinky, masculine-woman masturbation without my consent.

The anger was quickly replaced with internal hysteria. A maddening laugh shook through me. I tried not to laugh aloud. Was anyone else hearing this? What about the women on her level? Was she covered by the sheet? Did she have clothes on?

I laid in the top bunk begging my internal dialogue to turn up the volume. I planned the day.

Thwack, thwack.

I will eat BBQ for lunch. I will go grocery shopping for camping.

Squish squish.

Oh, fuck my life.

I have traveled to the far reaches of the globe, couch surfed like a champ, and it took Austin to legitimately keep it weird. It really does live up to its reputation.

At 7:20 a.m., the unattractive perpetrator with short hair left to go to the bathroom with her shower tote. I practically dove out of my bunk and onto the ground. I threw on my clothes and ate the hostel breakfast of peanut butter and jelly on a croissant, while reading the paper. A middle-aged man with a shaved head sat down at the table beside me.

"Good morning, how did you sleep?" he asked innocently, grabbing the sports section of the paper.

"It was a little hot in my room," I said. I put the paper up to my face, not wanting to erupt with laughter.

That was officially my weirdest sleeping accommodation adventure in all of my travels.

Keep it weird, Austin.

TRACI ANN

Last Night in Austin
9.19.14

For my final night in Austin I went back to the Spiderhouse Café, where I had watched the poetry slam, only this time for a couchsurfing event. It was supposed to be the weekly meet-up. I used to co-host the one held in New Orleans at Bacchanal Wine in the Bywater neighborhood. It was always a great group of positive, friendly travelers, so I wanted to catch that wave.

After I paid the bartender $6 for a Bulleit mule served in a hip mason jar, I made my way outside and breathed in the humid air. The courtyard was buzzing, I suppose in part from all the alcohol being consumed, but also the usual buzz of crowds of people grouped together, all talking about different topics. One of the groups had to be the couchsurfing meet up. But which one?

"Excuse me, do you know where the group of couchsurfers are?" I asked a bearded server passing me on the stairs.

"Down that way," he replied. He motioned me to a ragtag circle near the front of the courtyard. I went over and did a perimeter run around the group, eavesdropping on the collective conversation.

"This one time when I was backpacking through Thailand," sang into my ears and I knew I had found the right grouping of folks. However, I suddenly felt the need to be alone and just take in the scene.

I found a vintage two-seater metal rocker to sway on and sip my mule. I let the bite of the ginger sit on my tongue longer than necessary and paused every few sips to admire the funky courtyard. It was decked out with salvaged furniture and there was a canopy of old-school Christmas lights, the ones with huge bulbs, giving the yard a warm welcoming atmosphere. I took it in.

I am in Austin. I am traveling with all of my necessary belongings in my car through Texas and, I believe, to New Mexico. I have departed an old version of myself: a girl who used to live in New Orleans, compulsively date older men, work too many bartending gigs, and not speak up for herself when guys made her feel uncomfortable at work.

It felt uneasy, as it has every time, to let these ideas surface, but I did. Quietly, watching life on a Friday night in Austin unfold, from a vintage metal rocker made for two.

"Hi, are you a couchsurfer?" said a sweet voice. I looked up to locate the voice. An Asian guy wearing black, thick-rimmed glasses, and a backpack was standing in front of my metal rocker. On the perimeter scan, I had seen him in the middle of the group talking about Thailand.

"Yeah, I am here for the meet-up. Just taking things in," I said, swaying the rocker.

He opened his right hand, displaying his phone to me like a waiter displays the dessert tray. He smiled exuberantly, the phone lit up his thin moustache. "Look. A picture of surfing the North Shore in Hawaii last year," he said. The picture was gorgeous: a red surfboard cut through a crisp swell of ocean. It made me nostalgic for the waves I had surfed on the Pacific Rim.

"That's super cool," I replied, shifting in the rocker, "But why are you showing me a picture of surfing?" I continued, clearly looking bewildered.

He pointed to my magenta shirt with white lettering, "Your shirt says *love* and *surf.* Love is the universal sign for openness, so I came over," he said, beaming. Leave it to metaphysical Austin hipsters to pull a line on a girl like that.

This is Kevin. He is a photographer, web designer, self-published poet, and truly into metaphysics, not for the purpose of picking up pretty ladies in courtyards. Kevin is all about living effortlessly and in generosity. I told him about my travels and he thought it was fantastic; to travel with universal flow. Also known as, I don't know where I am going except west on Interstate 10. Totally Kevin, universal flow.

I loved his tranquil vibe and genuine smile, so I let him take me out of my introverted state in the metal rocker. We found a new spot, near a gazebo lit up by white mini lights, and talked non-stop for an hour.

I shook my head in admiration at his words. "Wait, so, this coming winter you are going to Central America to start a non-profit for kids?" I asked.

"Yep! I want to help educate children in the arts and the outdoors. Being outside is so healing, I want to create a space for that healing to happen," he replied.

I stirred my second Bulleit mule. "Weird, that's what I am good at—teaching kids outside."

"You could head up the program once I get it off the ground next spring, that is, if you aren't still driving around Texas!" We both laughed.

The synchronicities just kept rolling in. He started to speak about self-publishing and I focused all my attention on his youthful face.

"So where do you publish? I just opened an account on CreateSpace," I said proudly.

"Dude, KDP," Kevin replied.

I had no idea what he was talking about. "What is KDP?" I asked.

"Seriously? A travelin' writer lady like you doesn't use KDP?" He flashed a smile and tapped his phone quickly. "It is Kindle's e-publishing platform, you've got to get on it," Like earlier he fanned out his phone screen at me. It displayed all his poetry books published to date. "You can put your poetry out faster and in smaller digestives. It is a great balance of being able to speak truth and get paid here and there," he said.

"Wow, that *is* awesome," I said. External hard-drives full of half-finished prose suddenly felt within my grasp.

We shifted to sitting at a picnic table next to the gazebo and continued the conversation. He moved on to writing under a pen name.

"Use a pen name to protect yourself from the shadow side of things if it comes to that, also so you don't have to live up to your name as its identity currently is," he said.

Kevin challenged me. To produce my writing using a pen name, to dissolve my identity…to conceal all of my ego within the secret binding of the books I will soon produce.

Bullshit! Everyone must know it was me who created these masterpieces. My readers will need to know.

I scrunched my eyebrows at him, "But my readers will need to know it is me speaking to them," I countered.

"See, that's the test, to dissolve your concept of self totally, to write truth, and put it into the word anonymously, like a Chinese proverb."

I'm not Chinese, Kevin, but that does make a lot of sense.

The couchsurfer crowd thinned out as we continued the epic conversation of writing, abundance, and the universe. Kevin felt familiar and safe. We both seemed to glow in each other's radiance, our shared energy running super high. At some point we agreed to collaborate on both the non-profit and our conscious poetry, as if a literary agent had already done the legwork and we just happen to be having our business meeting at the Spiderhouse Café on a Friday night with all the undergrads of UT. He would call me when he needed help getting the educators together for his non-profit and I would stay in touch as I moved my writing towards self-publication.

We hugged goodnight and stepped apart. Kevin stood with his hands in prayer pose at his heart. Our smiles met.

"Peace, peace, peace" Kevin said, in the way you say, "Shanti, shanti, shanti" at a yoga ashram. I felt like Elizabeth Gilbert during the Pray part of her book, only my prayer involved rye whiskey and a chant under the Texas sky.

I took out a pen and small spiral notebook in my hostel bed that night. I started scribbling a list of pen names that sounded clever, just in case my ego was eclipsed sooner rather than later. I was blessed and alive with creative energy. My newest guardian angel on the trip, Kevin, was the one who had created all the buzzing energy of the courtyard for my last night in Austin.

Texas Tiny Houses

09.20.14

Goodbye, smelly masturbating girl in the hostel room.

Goodbye, Christina and your fancy solar home.

Goodbye, Kevin and your self-publishing/life-guru-ness.

Excitement electrified by body. More tiny homes today. Reservation to stay in one tonight. More alternative living craziness.

I rolled down all the windows in the car and let the strength of the breeze carry my goodbyes into the throes of life. I pointed the Chevy's mosquito-laden nose south down the asphalt county route. It is Saturday. I just had a wildly fun and random time in Austin and I am stoked to continue learning about other ways of providing shelter for myself sans mortgage.

Before I began this trip I had Googled "tiny homes in Texas," hoping to lace my journey with educating myself on burgeoning shelter interests. The SCADpads in Atlanta were my gateway drug. I wanted more. The hour came and went with the wind; I blasted through the small town of Luling and turned left on a dirt road labeled, "Texas Tiny Houses" with a spray painted sign. I parked, tossed up the sun cover on my windshield, and jumped into a group of twelve people for the guided tour. From all walks of life, we had all ventured to a random dusty place overlooking the I-10 to learn about tiny homes.

"Hey y'all! I'm Michelle and the COO here at Texas Tiny Homes, welcome to our property tour! Our owner, Darby, will join us soon," Michelle said. Her excessive green eyeliner matched her flowing sundress.

She was originally a film producer from Los Angeles. One day she woke up and didn't want all of her belongings anymore. She wanted to learn how to build her own small home. She found Darby and his book. Within a few years she was living in her rust red tiny house that sits on a hill at the TTH property. It was the first house we toured on site.

Michelle's bright green dress was like a flag to guide our tour. She led us to her small red home, opened the door, and ushered us in. "Well now don't be shy!" she said.

As we all walked in, a few of the men joked, "We aren't gonna all fit in there."

"Yes you are, come on in," Michelle coaxed them from the wood porch. The wives of the dubious men, with kids attached to every part of their bodies, gasped when we entered the small red house.

"This is *so* small! Where do you sleep?" One lady asked in a hushed tone, her eyes looking everywhere to locate the bedroom.

I pointed to the loft where Michelle's bed was. It felt odd to be with a crew who needed convincing about the tiny house thing, since all the folks I met in Atlanta gushed over the SCADpads.

The doubters wanted to participate, but as onlookers—voyeurs into the brave world others ventured. Michelle was the hero, venturing into the scary abyss of living with only one hundred and eighty square feet of life and no cable. Haters gonna hate.

"Yes, it does stay very cool in the summer heat," Michelle answered one of the women, pointing to a small AC unit deftly concealed under a sheer yellow curtain.

I was in love with Michelle's house, and we were only on the first house. The fact that it was made of all salvaged wooden components really grounded me. I could feel it tether into the earth, even though it was on piles. The different hues of wood were warm and cozy, unfettered with umpteen possessions, and well-kept with love and respect. Bliss floating within me, and I had the confirmation again, that yes, I wanted to brave the abyss of alternative living too. Ah, to be without ten million possessions, to have a shelter that is made using consciousness and artistic intentionality. Michelle's little red home was a dramatic reference point on my journey inward.

We moved onto the other homes and I continued to take photos to record the parts of each house that inspired me most; the lantern light fixtures, the stamped copper inside the shower, and the gorgeous Victorian-era wood from a demolished home in Detroit.

The whole site is an experiment in creating a sustainable living community, complete with a chapel, unique tiny homes, and a community bath house. Darby and his crew build the homes onsite in a large hanger and people pay top dollar to have them delivered all over the US and parts of Canada. We encountered him at the tour's stop at the chapel. He is the owner and builder of all ten acres of what I was viewing in Luling and he was damn proud. He stood tall—I guessed about 6'3"—and was tanned, with veins bulging from his sculpted yet scrawny arms.

"Well, come on in, folks, you're just in time for the sermon," he joked.

We filed into the chapel, all twelve of us, including the gasping mothers. We sat on the reclaimed pews inside the petite chapel and watched Darby walk in barefoot. I wondered how many nails he had stepped on. My sweaty legs stuck to the wood. Darby created a welcomed breeze when he walked past me to the lectern.

"Everything you see here would have gone in the landfill had me and my crew not grabbed it beforehand. My generation, the Baby Boomer generation, we done and screwed it up for the ones coming up." He pointed his wooden walking stick at me forcefully.

"We were so concerned with faster and easier, we neglected healthy and genuine. Now we have huge homes built with crappy, toxic materials, with carpets off-gassing and our babies continue to be poisoned every day." I looked at the babies still clinging to their mothers.

"Did you know how much bacteria and toxins your bed contains? The amount of chemicals that goes into making a mattress? There are beds out there made of safer materials now, but we don't want to spend the money. We want it cheaper. As long as there is the desire for cheap and large…we continue to riddle our lives and the lives of our children with disease!" His voice boomed. I felt like I really was at church. Darby was the pastor of progressive living. I wanted to shout an "Amen!"

"You all came here to tour these homes, I am guessing, because you are interested in alternative living, or at least curious, or you wouldn't be here. This isn't trendy, this isn't a fad; this is a radically different way to approach living life. To be intentional about space, the belongings we do have, and where they come from. It is our duty to do the best we can now to help heal the planet so this young lady's children can actually live on this Earth." He pointed at me again with his stick, finishing the speech.

Darby inhaled deeply and left the lectern, his bare feet thundering against the wood floor of the chapel. We all sat there staring at each other. I sniffled back tears, hoping nobody saw them. It was like he knew my thoughts.

The rest of the tour was about an hour. It was shaped by what Darby said. It wasn't just a bunch of gawkers putting the photos they took of the homes on Instagram with ridiculous hashtags, although I know I did. It was a tour of alternative homes shepherded through the lens of one man's passionate account of shelter. The homes were gorgeous, intricate, portable, and deftly assembled using one hundred percent reclaimed wood. There weren't any trips to Home Depot for studs. There were trips to Buffalo, NY to claim the remains of old gutted homes that were being sacrificed for newer, more spacious condos made of particle board and toxic shit.

The heat of the day subsided as all the families piled back into their minivans and zipped up the I-10, back to their normal lives and mortgaged homes. It was just me, Darby, Michelle, a few builder guys, and a cute black and brown wiener dog named Needlenose. She rolled in the grass, opening her belly to me and wagged her tail playfully. I used both hands and rubbed her belly.

"Now that the tour is done, let me go get the towels for your stay and I'll put them in the Blue Moon," Michelle said, and then ran off to set up the Blue Moon. That was the third or fourth home we had seen on the tour. My home for one tiny, short night.

I drove back down the dirt access road and into Luling for a late afternoon pick-me-up. The only place that was open was a Subway at the main intersection. I opted for two double-chocolate chip cookies and a cherry coke. My body reveled in the sugar rush I very rarely give it. I knew I would crash hard in a few hours, but I didn't care. Such a silly thing to do after Darby's sermon, placing sugar toxins into my body. I could feel the zing of energy and remembered why it is so hard to treat your body, home, and life with respect via holistic measures. Because things like junk food, casual sex, and cheap tequila all taste and feel so good in the moment. In the moment, the ecstasy of the high is too high. We are blind to the inevitable crashing low.

I contemplated the idea of a long game as I rode my sugar high. A long game, three mental moves out on the chess board, a future plan. How do you develop a long game and live fiercely in the present? For junk food consumption and all of the other usual suspects. What does a long game look like and what are the action steps? Even once you have the plan, action is always the hardest damn part of it.

By 4 p.m., Michelle escorted me on the dirt path to my temporary tiny home, the Blue Moon. The cookies and soda had made me crash and I felt like shit. My head hurt, and I regretted my decision. *Gotta work on the long game*, I laughed at myself.

Staying in the tiny house was amazing. I watched the sunset off the front porch, examined the cacti in my front "lawn" up close. I had never really seen a cactus up close before, so I did a full assessment, placing my face just shy of the spines to get a good look. The house stayed cool, just like Michelle's had, by way of the window-unit A/C and the open floor plan. The sunset spilled onto the hardwood, making the baby blue colored walls glow. The house was one hundred and sixty square feet, had a bathroom adjoined to it, a bottom floor, and a loft where a queen-sized bed was. There was no kitchen inside, but if it was truly my tiny house, I would have devoted the back left corner to my kitchen.

I nestled under the covers of the queen bed early, admiring my surroundings before turning out the light. The height of the loft surprised me. In the middle of the pitch I could almost stand straight up. Contentment-induced sleep overcame me within minutes of laying down.

The next morning, the sunrise woke me, filling up the small window in the loft. I stretched and rolled around in the bed of the Blue Moon joyfully. *I can totally picture myself living this way! I have a long game.* In my long game I envisioned a group of my closest friends and I living together, on a plot of land, with several tiny homes, chickens, a garden, and hippie pants. Lots of multi-colored hippie pants.

AUTHENTIC. SEXY. TRUTH.

Part Four: West Texas

Wilderness begins in the mind.
- *Edward Abbey*

TRACI ANN

A Walk in My Wilderness
09.21.15

After a crappy yet comforting breakfast of Subway's steak, egg and pepper-jack, I forced myself on the interstate headed west. The good vibes of the tiny home stay wore off fast when I saw the blue and red Interstate sign. I-10 East, turn left. I-10 West, turn right. The stretch of road from Fort Stockton to Big Bend National Park, the actual road to the park, was still 130 miles in front of me. Yet, for some cosmic reason, my body registered this as the point of no turning back.

Big Bend. Big mindfuck. Big change.

I let out an audible whimper when I turned right. Apparently, seven hours further west meant I could never go back to New Orleans, or any other place I previously inhabited for that matter.

Sadness swept over me. I thought about Steph. About all the times she said she would deal with things at work. Then she didn't do a damn thing to truly protect me. Sure, she let me rent out her back room, but she didn't stand up for a fellow woman at work. Betrayed as I felt, I had to go west. My life in the east was now dead. I could continue crying about it internally all I wanted, but my old life was dead. The woman I once knew, the girl who lived in her boss's back room and rolled around in the grass with a charming music manager...she was now dead.

My body and brain are trying to help my soul grieve. To let the precious girl inside cry for what she tossed out the window five hundred miles back—old shrapnel of herself. The bullets of life tore apart the girl I once knew. One month ago, she got shot. Pieces of her exploded outward onto the horizon. They flew so far, I decided to go in search of them near New Mexico.

I drove five hours on the I-10, stopping only to get gas and pee. Whenever the emotional demons gained on me, I pressed the gas pedal harder. The speed limit opened up to eighty-five, I gunned it, and the Chevy's engine roared with power. Windows up. Windows down.

Radio on. Radio off. I couldn't shake the feeling of being followed. I desperately wanted to get to Big Bend and set up camp.

Five hours came and went. I turned onto Route 385 out of Fort Stockton, and some serious two-lane country opened up. My jaw was down, and so was my window, for most of the final two and a half hours before officially entering one of the most piercingly desolate national parks in the US.

Maybe it is an East Coast thing, but the west is fucking *huge*. It got scary and intimidating really fast; the open blue sky made my heart flutter with a twinge of panic. I thought of my bed in my storage unit. *I don't want to camp anymore, I want my bed, I want a home.* I was freaking out a little. I had not tried out my freshly-purchased camp stove yet, or made sure my tent worked properly, I just knew it was in the trunk. Everything I needed to camp was decidedly inside the car, except my gumption.

Why do wide open spaces, vast swaths of public land, make us feel vulnerable? Why do we all work so hard to create mega cities that we densely populate, moan about how much of a clusterfuck it is, and then drive halfway across the southern US to get to a wide-open space—only to run away screaming?

I closed in on Big Bend around 5:30 p.m. The terrain transitioned from arid scrubland along the I-10 to a very unforgiving, desert place. Roadrunners scampered across the highway. They were shorter than I pictured. I had hoped they would be purple and taunting a wild coyote. The plateaus that flanked the interstate had morphed into jagged outcroppings of reddish crags and undulating mountains. I entered the park, pulled into the Persimmons Ranger Station parking lot, and went to go ask for directions—or, perhaps, to ask for general life guidance. There was only one road, but I still wanted a verbal confirmation that yes, I was indeed on the right path. I pictured the nice ranger man, in his green park outfit, shaking my hand saying, "Yes, little lady, you have come to the right place indeed." He would tip his hat in a southern gentlemanly way, and I would drive further into the park, confident in my choice to camp in the remote desert.

This did not happen. A white jeep Wrangler covered in mud blasted into the parking lot, reverberating some Red Hot Chili Peppers song off the sandstone mountains. It stopped abruptly, and a young guy jumped out, beating me up the sidewalk to the ranger who was standing at the outdoor park map. I walked up behind him, ready to push him out of the way, and then observed I couldn't even see the ranger around this guy's broad shoulders.

"Yeah well, if you want to do the South Rim Loop, you need your backcountry permit, young man," the ranger said, wagging his finger at the tall jerk.

"I got 'em right here," he replied. His deep voice had a southern twang to it.

I pretended to be engrossed in my own route planning by staring at the outdoor map. They kept talking about backcountry trails and water drop off points. I was out of my league; I didn't even know if my new camp stove worked. I jumped back in the car and rallied passed the white jeep with its outdoorsy roof rack container. I am *so* not outdoorsy enough for this. That guy is ready. I am a carpooling hobo who happened to have bought camping equipment in Atlanta.

Whatever.

I kept driving. Another forty-five minutes. I didn't see a car the whole time until I reached Panther Junction's empty parking lot. I was hopeful a ranger here would give me verbal treats of comforting confirmation that all in the world was right and I made a good choice to drive thirty minutes shy of the Mexican border.

Nope. Closed.

I was leaving to bravely follow the signs to my campground when the guy in the jeep rolled into the closed station. *What a butthead*, I thought, sneering at him from behind my steering wheel.

I cranked my tunes upon seeing the sign for the Chisos Basin Campground. Six miles. *I got this.* Halfway in, the Chevy hemmed and hawed at the sight of switchbacks and signage of steep grades, the one where it looks like the truck is falling off the yellow cliff. I hate those signs. Three tears escaped my eyeballs and streamed down my cheek. I was losing gumption. I loved all things outdoors and I asked the universe for mountains, but what I forgot that what comes with mountains is driving on them.

I do not enjoy driving machines up and down hills. My heart raced down the first grade. I couldn't remember how to slow down with less effort from the car. Two more. I could smell my brakes. Panic set in, though I could see my campground below.

"Bring it to a lower gear, brake until 10 mph, let off the brake, bring it up to 25 or so, brake again. Take your time, you're doing great." My dad's calm voice swirled in my head. The winter I turned sixteen, dad took me driving in our red minivan on the slick local hills so I could learn to downshift on complicated terrain.

I found the 3-2-1 display on my dash and popped the car into two. It immediately slowed down and relaxed. So did I. Just then, the guy in the white freaking jeep came barreling around the corner behind me. *Ass*. I found a vista spot and pulled off to let him go in front of me. He waved in his rearview and I slowly but steadily followed him into camp.

I somehow got in front of him within the campground and parked the car in front of the bathrooms. I saw a nice little spot with flat gravel adjacent to the bathroom. The whole basin was wrapped up in the red Chisos Mountains. White jeep guy exited the bathroom. I could feel his gaze upon me. I scoped out my site, kicking the gravel around, and heard big footsteps behind me.

"Hey there! Find a good spot yet?" he asked.

I turned around, ready to wallop him. Instead I admired his brown fedora, blue eyes, and the way his chest muscles pushed out his red shirt.

"I think this one!" I exclaimed. Anxious he might take my spot, I yanked my tent out of its box and chucked it into the gravel, claiming my land.

"Cool, what's your name?" he asked, indifferent to my rude gesture.

"Traci."

He took off his hat reflexively and held out his hand, "Jake." His hand was warm and big. "Are you traveling alone?" he asked, exposing a slight gap in between his front teeth.

I was hesitant at first, and deliriously tired from the near nine hours of being in my car. "Yep, I'm here alone, traveling from New Orleans.

Well, I'm moving," I shifted my stance, "I wanted to try camping by myself for the first time," I sputtered.

His eyes were wide in curiosity. "Cool, wow, you picked quite the place for it to be your first time to solo," I watched his blue eyes look me up and down quickly. "But you look like a girl who won't have any trouble," he said, giving me a quick wink.

A red rush of attraction and confidence pulsed through me. The mutual attraction throbbed between us.

"Well, I'm going to go check this site out down the hill, we should drink some tea together later. I packed some extra if you'd like," Jake said. And with that, he bounced down the hill with his backpack, disappearing from my line of sight.

Wow. Did I just score a date in one of the most isolated parts of Texas? I kicked a few rocks around in affirmation. I am an outdoor-badass-sexy-woman-made-of-moxie. Bam.

Jake came back over five minutes later. He sort of pranced. It was cute.

"You put that thing up fast!" he said, pointing to my tent.

"Ha, yeah, well I used to take groups of fifteen kids on overnight camping trips. I got used to putting tents up fast," I said.

"So I found a site with a killer overlook and a covered picnic table. I am only gonna be here one night with my hammock, then headed to the backcountry. Do you want to pitch your tent on the site with me and we can split the cost then you can stay?" he offered in the sweetest tone.

But I wanted my splendid, desolate loneliness I had traveled so far from populated cities to reach. Now a random cute man wants to be all up in my campsite? My mental chatter paused, and my heart spoke her words quickly, "Yeah! That'd be great."

"Awesome, we can just pick up your tent, I'll help you carry it," he said, grabbing one side of my pup tent. We carried it five sites down to the one he had offered.

I get anxious around new guys that I actually like. I fidget and pretend to be busy. I hurried around in and out of my car putting food in the bear box and locating my camp stove and red propane tank. The sun was setting off some gorgeous colors of red and bluish orange against the mountains. Jake was in his hammock simply taking it all in.

"Come over here for a minute...you're gonna miss the sunset," he said, patting the empty space next to him in the hammock.

Just like that. In the middle of nowhere. I slide into a hammock with adorable Jake from New Mexico. Jake who works for Halliburton and does fracking. Jake who has an older sister who lives in Austin. Our thighs warm pressed against each other, we sat and watched the sunset. It was so easy to be around this guy, like we had camped a million times together, and this was just another sunset we shared. I was happy and less scared of Big Bend with Jake around.

In the remaining hours before bed, he watched me commit many firsts. All in the dark. The first time cooking with my camp stove, the first time figuring out how to get boiling water from a pot to a container of freeze dried beef mac 'n' cheese using a spork and a lighter. All the while he didn't do it for me, like many men would. Men I used to date did it for me. Men I used to work with did it for me. They would patronize; assuming I couldn't do it. Jake knew I could do it on my own.

"There you go, just figure it out, I'm not gonna do it for ya, that's part of the adventure," he said, grinning in the glare of my headlamp. We laughed together as I gingerly moved the pot of boiling water over the bag of food, using my bandana as a hot mitt.

Marry me, please? A man who offers me tea and *empowerment? Sold.*

We drank his two bags of chamomile tea in the darkness, looking up at an endless sky of stars. Neither of us knew which star was which, but we knew it was pretty fucking spectacular to be standing under them.

I said goodnight to Jake, and he told me he liked my glasses. I wear thick square glasses before bed, after I take out my contacts. Few people see me in them because I don't really like the way they look. I look like a librarian in boy shorts, and the prescription is outdated. I snuggled into my sleeping bag. The mountain air was cold but my heart was warm with gratitude.

Big Bend is a giant desert wilderness. Today it felt like I entered my own wilderness, the wilderness of my mind. It is as endless as Big

Bend. It has mountains, roadrunners, and stars that look like they are melting towards the earth.

The enormity of your own wilderness is enough to make you want to cry in fear, shame, and happiness. You want to fight it, to hide, but at the same time you must pitch your tent there…in the wilderness of yourself.

I did that today. I pitched my tent, for the first time, in my wilderness. And, surprisingly, I had company to kindly offer me some verbal confirmations and tea. The wilderness is so big, yet because we are not separate, we are truly never alone on this journey.

Thanks for walking into my wilderness with me, Jake.

TRACI ANN

Desert Frolic
09.22.14

This morning I woke up to the clatter of Jake fixing himself breakfast. His little aluminum pot clanged ever so slightly against the prongs of his lightweight backpacking stove. I emerged from my tent most likely a hot mountain girl mess. I felt like one. My back hurt, and my hair was standing up on one end. I unzipped the tent to reveal the towering Chisos, covered in a gray morning fog. The air was cold still; it nipped my face with a refreshing bite.

"Morning!" Jake said. He was chipper. Clearly a morning person.

"Morning," I grumbled.

He clapped his hands together over his aluminum pot, pressing his lips together. "Well, just breakfast and then I'm off. Already dropped my water on the other side of Emory Peak," he said.

"Wow, geesh, you're way ahead of me," I replied, admiring his pecs once more, this time outlined in a gray hiking shirt.

My stomach grumbled. Jake had been awake since like 5 a.m. It was now 8 a.m. I felt like a camping poser. But a poser who knew how to use her damn camping stove. I busted it out with enthusiasm and revved up the propane for coffee and maple sugar instant oatmeal.

"Is that instant coffee with hazelnut creamer?" he asked in disbelief as the smell wafted at his face from my mug.

I looked up at him coyly, "Yep, do you want some?"

"Yes!" he presented his tin mug for me to fill.

We broke camp. Jake all packed up for his two-day trip, and my official solo site was all tidy. We followed each other to the Panther Junction welcome center to get our actual park passes, and his backcountry permit. On the scary road down, my tire gauge light came on. *Fuck. Tire pressure low. Shit.* What does that mean when you are on the mountain switchbacks?

It means you keep going and pray, I think. That's what I did anyways. And then tell your new backcountry-camping boyfriend that you have low tire pressure. I beeped my horn feverishly at Jake in front of me. He made a right into a nearby lodge parking lot.

I tried to play it cool. Pretending the ten or so rapid horn beeps did not come from my car.

"You okay?" he asked with concern in his eyes.

"Oh, ah, yeah—my tire pressure light came on and I don't have a pump," I said. We peered around the side of the white hood, examining the tires. The left front tire leaned down.

"Oh no worries, I have a heavy-duty bike pump in my car that should do the trick," Jake said and opened the back of his jeep. He rummaged through the backseat and then dashed over to my car. "I used to work at Discount Tire, you know, I know a thing or two about tires." He was so adorable. He stood on either side of the bike pump, securing it under his hiking boots, and began pumping up and down. He pumped my tires one at a time, making sure each one was primed and ready for its day trip.

"Thank you so much, Jake," I said, watching him pump. Up. Down. Up. Down.

I wondered what he was like in bed. What other ways could he pump? My dirty daydream was cut in half by a group of young guys laughing at us as they passed by.

"Good thing I like to pump," Jake said earnestly. Thankfully I caught myself from blurting out any forward comments that were tossing around in my horny mind.

I bet he rocks in bed. Hell, I bet he's even better in a tent.

It took forty-five minutes for Jake to convince the park ranger at Panther Junction to issue him his backcountry pass. By the time he was ready, permit in hand, I had learned about mountain lions and the

Mexican Blue Jay thirty times. We walked outside together, back into the lifting morning fog.

"Sorry that took so long, two people died in the backcountry on this route last summer and they wanted to make sure I had enough experience," he said.

"It's fine. But, are you sure you'll be okay out there?" I asked, trying not to sound nervous. I was still getting acclimated to the daunting front country wilderness of Big Bend, and he was heading into the harsh, overgrown backcountry where people died of dehydration.

"Yes ma'am, I'll be fine," he replied. "Well, so what do you say, we meet each other in Terilingua on Wednesday night for a beer? Hopefully I won't die out there, and you can tell me what it's like to ride in a rowboat across the Rio Grande to Mexico," he said playfully.

"You got it," I said.

We took a selfie, exchanged numbers, and, just like it never happened, Jake was off. My wilderness boyfriend was off into the sunset—or rather, the morning monsoon of late summer in the desert.

I waited the rain out, eating fruit in my car in preparation for the day hike I had chosen: the Chimneys trail, a five-mile roundtrip "moderate" hike on the desert floor of the park. I picked it because the end promised two enormous stacked piles of red rocks that looked like chimneys. The picture from the visitor center brochure looked pretty.

I got on the road and headed west for sixteen miles through the park, slowing navigating hills and, bit by bit, gaining confidence in my ability to drive my Chevy correctly on hilled terrain. I got to the trailhead at high noon. It was cloudy and the idea of a two-and-a-half-hour desert hike at the worst possible time of day didn't really cross my mind. I was ready for my first solo desert hike. I downed a peanut butter and jelly sandwich, drank half a Nalgene of blue Powerade, and got all packed up. Mini survival kit, water bottle and orange in the daypack. Lightweight socks and hiking boots on the feet. Here we go. I took a picture of the trail marker and began the flat walk. A walkabout through the desert with Mexico in the distance.

The desert is so untouched, so ruthless in its beauty. Yellow and purple wildflowers begged for my attention while the looming Chisos convinced my eyes to look up. Little rustling noises amidst the cactuses and rocky terrain made me scan a ten-foot perimeter around me every minute or so. I was in bear, mountain lion, and rattlesnake country. *Walk, walk, walk. Think, think, think.* Stop, listen to the wind, take in the fresh air. It smelled so pungent with wildflowers and moisture. I felt invigorated as I approached the chimneys. It was so powerful to stand in the desert alone. I hadn't seen anyone all day; the volume of silence was magnificent. Profoundly lonely and scary; anything could happen. I scrambled up one of the chimney's bases and took a few timed photos. Pensive Traci on the boulder outcropping. Cool Traci looking like she is totally fine being in the desert alone. *I can be whoever I want.*

I sat on the rocks above the desert for a while pondering things like, *what happens if I see a mountain lion? Is that Santa Elena Canyon in the distance? Should I eat my Clifbar now or later? Will a bear smell it and come over for a sample?*

Around one o'clock I inhaled a final calming breath and triumphantly began the journey back. The clouds had totally receded by the time I was halfway back. The desert was a hot motherfucker. My neck sizzled, my scalp baked underneath my faded Patagonia hat. I could see my car off in the distance, noticed my water was less than half full, and thought of the people who had died of dehydration in the backcountry last summer. My pace quickened and so did my heart rate. Slight panic surrounded me, the desert grew crowded with anxiety. Dizziness manifested out of nowhere and I staggered for a moment across the trail.

My brain switched to my Wilderness First Responder skills. *Ok, stop. Take off your hat, let your head lose some of the heat. Three deep breathes. You are fine, Traci.* I collected myself in the desert delirium and continued to finish out the trail. Every time I became nervous that I might pass out I would count my steps. One-two-three-four-five-six-seven-eight. Repeat. I saw the trailhead in the distance and a wave of bliss crashed on top of me. My water had been empty for a while. I chalked my lack of better preparedness up to novice excitement. I raced to the car, turned on the A/C and quickly filled my water with the Powerade mix, knowing my body was craving a fix of sugars and salt.

I chomped on the orange like an animal. I took ten huge breathes to push the stress out of my system. I looked through the pictures I'd taken before driving back to my campsite.

Dusk came, and I watched the sunset from my covered picnic table. A pinch of longing for my new camp companion stung me. I wanted to sit in the hammock again, with our warm thighs pressed together and recount the tales of the day. Give thanks that we were both alive. Alas, it was just me and my chili beef mac 'n' cheese dinner. I killed the meal fast and then sat in my camp chair clutching a cup of ginger tea as I watched the first stars of the evening show up.

I made a wish on the first shooting star that raced the sky. I also gave thanks for my luck in the desert, congratulating myself on receiving the first badge of outdoor badass honor: completing a solo hike. It might not seem like a lot to others, but when it is your own personal wilderness, it means life and death. Today I lived. Today I grew. Filled with inspiration from the day, and contemplative from the vast night sky, I took out my journal and began to write. A story appeared in my mind's eye. I penned it in the red glow of the headlamp.

The Travelers Bucket

The traveler's journey is a bucket of empty, most times. It feels lonely and curious. But, that's the only way to keep the bucket. The traveler must keep the bucket devoid of anything she acquires—be it material or otherwise. So it can be available for the contents of other people's lives. The bucket then is truly not a bucket...it is a caldron. Empty, waiting to be made a vessel for the life soup. Soup of the souls. Fellow travelers contribute their precious ingredients from their packs; stories of love lost, trials, hard decisions, friendships and empathy for the traveler and her empty caldron.

These fellow vagabonds no longer have traveling caldrons heated by camp stoves; their kettles are on cozy hot flames burning bright inside their homes. Homes which are located deeply in the seat of their own observer. The traveler accepts magical abundance and over the rickety camp stove, she lights the flame. She shelters it gently from the

125

wind and tosses all of the ingredients in. The stars twinkle ever so preciously in the night sky and she feels in the company of the like-minded wayfarers. The soup of journey is bubbling in her deep cauldron; the smells of walk-abouts of the other travelers contribute to her story. The cold. The cold starry night on the high desert serves her. The soup is ready and she looks up to ladle the journey into the bowls of the gracious volunteers of adventure. All there is though, is black night.

A full pot of everyone's life and no one to share it with? Where have they all gone? Can she bring herself to ingest the others? To absorb into her blood-stream the contents of all the parties? All her angels dance in the stars, happy to have guided the traveler with her empty bucket-caldron.

She sips quietly the soup of souls, knowing contentedly that the traveler is never alone and life is always too full with glorious abundance.

Hitting the Wall
09.23.14

We all hit the wall. Get slammed into it. Pushed up against it by an invisible hand throttling our throats.

When you hit the wall, you know it. The wall is the pain of the in between, the pain of transition from this present moment, to that present moment. When previous life events begin to shed away like old skin off your worn feet, and the new life is made blurry by your tears. Pain, agony, darkness, and anger beyond belief...these shadows taunt you at the wall, blocking the way out. The wall is your ego putting up an impromptu block saying: you shall not pass...until you face your shit.

This is the wall. And the wall ate me for lunch today.

I went to the Chisos Mountain Lodge in the morning to use the free wi-fi. I bought a cup of coffee and soup that was too salty. For a good hour I felt normal; doing the weekly traveler business of emailing, checking Facebook, and banking. The banking triggered the wall. It socked me like a crisp right hook to the jaw. *I am still traveling on this exodus from New Orleans and I am running out of money!*

Terror, and then seething anger obliterated my gorgeous view of the Chisos. I took a moment and let it explode. *Fuck you, NORP. It is all your fault I am out here in a giant national park scrounging by, camping, driving down steep roads I don't know, and forced into my own wilderness. I don't want to be here and I don't want to continue. Why did this happen? I liked my job, why did you do this NORP? Why, why, why?*

I stared at my bank account page for a while. Tears flowing. Purposeless. The waitress avoided my eyes when she refilled my coffee mug. Feeling wrecked, I didn't want to continue the trip. I hit the wall and I did not want to keep traveling. I wanted to stop, turn around, and run to the nearest thing that would give me comfort. I even thought of driving to New York to my parents' home.

It raged deeper. *Fuck you, storage unit with all of my things! I hate you, things! I despise the $80 I give you every month to store my shit. I don't have anywhere to call home yet. It. Is. All. Your. Fault. Storage. Unit.*

And deeper. *Fuck you Marcus. Fuck you so hard. That is what you wanted, wasn't it? For us to fuck? Or at least a little get together; a little side item to complement your fragmented marriage. Why did you do that? Those late night pictures. Requests for photos of me at 2 a.m. Most likely so you could jack off to them. I hope you jacked off all over your wife's pillow and woke her up, you cheating motherfucker. Why did you think it was okay to confess your love to me...to say you were so attracted to me, time and time again? We worked together. We worked so well together. I trusted you. Why did you break that? You fell through thin ice and I wish you would die under there, a cold death that nobody hears.*

Why are you so mad? Marcus countered in my mind's replay of things.

Did you really just ask me why, Marcus? My thoughts were a train that had been viciously de-railed. *Because harassing me at work, causing me to feel like I was on eggshells, incessantly verbalizing lustful intentions when I told you to stop was wrong! It is still wrong even though I am in a national park with mountains to shelter me from you. You raped me with words at work. So did Reggie and Darius. Rape of the tongue. There is no rape kit for that. No way to prove that words hurt desperately. You crossed my most sacred boundaries, and I am forever changed. The disbelief and hurt still stings on the back left side of my tongue about once a week. I am trying to heal the hole you put in my heart with your words. From Darius's comments about my sexy outfits on Instagram. From Stephanie's lack of action. What does the healing look like for verbal rape? Can I honor the sexy goddess I know myself to be in the future days and not be worried this will happen again?*

I slumped in the chair, my coffee was now cold and nasty. Today I hit the wall. It was the wall of past hurt. Recent trauma. Of a dwindling bank account.

How do you get past the wall?

I looked out upon the grandeur of Big Bend from the mountain lodge and took a moment to ground. To notice where I actually was. So consumed in my small mind, I was viewing the situation as an enormous failure. I resigned, committed to driving to nowhere, and now I was successfully in the middle of nowhere. But that was the goal, to get to nowhere. So in fact, I had accomplished my mind's goal. Maybe the nowhere—the desert of uncertainty—is where we say, "Okay, let us begin."

I think there are two ways to get past the wall. The wall that plants itself straight up on the middle of your newest life path. You either take baby steps around it—healing slowly, and slowly inching around the side near the shoulder of the road. Or you dynamite that concrete motherfucker. You give it to that wall so hard, she wishes concrete could scream because it hurt so good. I am choosing the latter option, with a sprinkling of baby steps to muffle the screaming noise as I walk on.

I looked out on the Window Trail from the Chisos lodge. The window is a pointy overlook, a rock window, where you can look out onto the canyon lands of Mexico and beyond. Two worlds, separated by a wall of rock, with a triangular window. I looked at it in the distance and squinted, trying to see the future pieces of my life. The rage subsided, but I still couldn't totally see beyond the damn wall.

As much as I try to fight with my life, try to blame the situation on everything and everyone else, it does no good. Marcus doesn't give a fuck anymore, nor does anyone I used to work with. The women of Human Resources don't care that I am living out of my car.

Blame placed anywhere is wasted time and energy. As Elizabeth Gilbert said, "Send them love and light, and then drop it." I sat with my too-salty soup for what seemed like hours, but the forgiveness was not ready to be given.

Where's the dynamite? I do truly want to keep going. Just get this fucking wall out of my way.

TRACI ANN

Change of Plans, Fort Stockton
09.24.14

The plan—the ever-so-meticulously calculated plan—was to wake up early today, break down my camp, and drive over to the Rio Grande side of the park. It was my final day in Big Bend and I wanted to do the Boquillas border crossing into Mexico. This is a border spot in the park which was closed the past ten or so years since 9/11. It just recently reopened. I heard Boquillas was a dusty small town, with a windblown family-owned cantina that served beers and lunch. My big final plan was to cross the Rio Grande in a rowboat operated by a Mexican national, get my passport stamped, drink a beer in Mexico, and then drive two hours to Alpine to sleep for the night. And then skip on down to Marfa, twenty miles west of Alpine, to attend a three-day music festival I booked haphazardly in Atlanta using the reason of YOLO.

Well, dear reader, we make plans and watch them unravel every time. The only plan that seems to be somewhat reliable is the one between a woman's ovaries and the moon. And sometimes even these celestial bodies can't sync up as planned. Lesson being: plans change, don't pout.

I was all packed up, fed, and the dishes done by 8:30 a.m. I was an accomplished car camper. My first solo camp behind me, I was no longer a dehydrated dinner virgin. I shut the trunk and jumped in the car, ready for the border crossing event. I went to start the Chevy's engine and it was dead. Super dead. Like I must-have-left-the-damn-door-slightly-open-all-night dead. I wanted to cry again. I began to pout.

Not today! I am supposed to go to Mexico and then brag on Instagram about how cool and adventurous my roaming lifestyle is. I tried the key again. Nothing. But Chevy! We are on top of a mountain...why *now*?

Because plans change.

I looked up from the driver's seat in faint alarm. There was a guy about my age packing up his car, too. I approached him quickly.

"Hey! Do you have jumper cables? My car won't start," I said, putting on my best damsel in distress pouty face.

"Yeah I do," he said.

For an hour, Arash—a stiff, aspiring doctor in the making—tried to give CPR to my car. I had never jumped a car before, so I asked the doctor the steps as we went along.

"Red goes with red, then you put the black cable on a part of your car that is grounded," he pointed to an arbitrary bolt.

"Why did you put it on that bolt?" I asked innocently.

He looked at me with frustration, "I don't know, somebody told me that's where you put the black cable."

Typical doctor.

It took us thirty minutes to realize we weren't even charging the car because the red cable kept slipping off the bolt on my crusty old battery. Sparks crackled as we reset the cables a tad and the dash blinked the red charging icon. I ignited the engine and felt the dread melt off me. I would live. I didn't have to camp in Big Bend for the rest of my life. The dynamite had exploded the wall, and now I could drive across the rubble. I thanked Arash for his time, and he quickly left for Houston.

Before I drove down the mountain, I stopped at the Chisos lodge once more. Jake had parked his jeep there; it was the South Rim Loop entrance point. I searched my glove box for a pen that worked. I scribbled on a small piece of paper: *Headed to Alpine instead of Terilingua, meet me there for a beer?* I pinned the crumbled note inside the driver's side door handle. I hoped it didn't blow away.

By the time I let the car charge, and got back down to Panther Junction, it was nearing eleven. Even if I did get to the border crossing in an hour, which was the allotted time according to the park map, I didn't even know if I could cross the river. Due to the recent strong rainfall, the park had been advising people against canoeing any sections of the river. I couldn't imagine the park rangers would advise jumping in a rickety rowboat with the Mexican nationals either. I didn't feel like risking it all for an overpriced tourist beer and social media bragging rights, so my plans changed again. Instead of getting my passport stamped at the border, I got it stamped in the visitor center. I leaned my weight into the ink stamp, depressing it to my actual US passport. The stamp was bold and proud: *Big Bend National Park. 9.25.14.*

I got back in the recharging Chevy and started the hour drive out of the park heading northeast, the opposite way of Terilingua. I studied the mountains and desert not only with awe, but also with a newfound respect and warm familiarity. The home of my first solo camp.

Now that the plan to border cross was expired I did some on-the-fly planning. Somewhere between eating BBQ in Austin and walking around the desert I managed to secure a phone interview with the wilderness adventure therapy company that Todd Matthews had referred me to. My last day in Austin I fired off a red-hot resume and a cover letter with Todd's name in the first sentence. By the time I had gotten to the tiny homes in Luling, the field coordinator at Compass Wilderness had emailed me back. They wanted to schedule a phone interview, as my resume spoke for itself, and Todd raved about me.

Yes! Direction, a plan, potential purpose on the journey to nowhere.

We scheduled the appointment for early morning Thursday, to knock it out before I headed to Marfa for the Trans Pecos Music Festival. The plan evolved from border crossing into Mexico for beers to backtracking north two hours to Fort Stockton where I last had cell phone reception.

Fort Stockton has many motels. The population is about eighty-five hundred, according to a battered city limits sign, and it has a drive-through discount beverage center. I checked into the Budget Inn at 1:30 p.m. and rapidly regrouped my life in the motel room. I shaved my legs, washed all the dried hiker sweat out of my hair, laundered my nasty clothes, and scoured Compass Wilderness' website to prepare for tomorrow's phone interview. I called a few of my best girlfriends and strongest supporters of the "Traci goes west" movement to rally. It worked; my sense of being a badass wayfaring lady returned.

My phone chimed a text message while I was folding my laundry on the king size motel bed.

Jake: *I made it from the backcountry! I got the note you shoved in my car door. Headed to Alpine for that beer* ☺

Shit. I changed places again and didn't tell him.

Traci: *Wait! Don't go to Alpine, I am so sorry to skip around, I got a job interview for an outdoor company in Utah, I needed cell phone reception so I came up to Fort Stockton.*

Jake: *No worries. That's on my way to San Antonio, can I come by and take you to dinner? I'd still love a burger and a beer like we had planned.*

Traci: *Sure! That'd be great.*

Three hours later my campground playmate found me in Fort Stockton. I somehow managed to score both a job interview and a date with my rugged outdoorsy pretend boyfriend. Take that, dynamited wall! I did my best to fluff out my layered hair before Jake arrived. I also tried to locate a more attractive outfit than my dank hiker clothes. He picked me up in the Jeep and we went to a nearby bar and grill. We ate bacon burgers, drank Coronas, and he teased me about not crossing the border.

"It wouldn't have taken that long! You should've done it," he bantered. "But, judging by the looks of that motel room, you really do have a lot going on, it is like a headquarters in there."

I'm glad Jake understood this nomadic goddess ruled her world remotely. "But the car died!" I insisted.

"I know, I'm just messing with you," he said, jostling my knee with his hand.

"So what was the backcountry like?" I asked, squaring my body at his underneath the table.

"Oh man! It was hard. Amazing though." He took a huge bite of his burger. "I saw a bear on the trail from Emory Peak."

"What did you do? Were you scared?"

"A little. I made a lot of noise like they tell you to, and it just ran off," he said, ordering a second Corona. "Towards the end it got a little hairy though. I underestimated the water I needed, so I had to filter water from puddles."

"Are you serious, Jake! Shit, that's some crazy stuff," I said.

"What about you? How was the Chimneys trail?" he asked.

"Ah, it was rad. I saw some jackrabbits and the quiet of the trail was insane," I said dipping my fries in a pile of ketchup.

He dropped me off at my motel room and hugged me, saying, "I didn't expect to meet anyone on this trip, let alone the coolest girl ever." He held me for an extra moment. "If you get this job in Utah I would come visit you…even if you didn't and you worked somewhere else, I want to visit you."

I wanted to kiss him. I wanted him to come into the dingy motel room and throw me down on the bed; to know the other kinds of pumping he was capable of. The moment hung in the air for a minute and then it passed just like the plans of the day.

"Well, stay in touch, okay?" I said, nudging my hip into him.

"I will, I wanna hear how the interview goes," he replied, standing in the motel room's doorway in an undecided fashion.

"Okay."

"Alright, pretty lady," he said, beginning to turn towards his Jeep.

"Drive carefully. Are you awake enough to drive?" I asked, half hoping he needed to nap in my motel bed.

"Nah, I'll be just fine."

"Well, thanks for everything, Jake, really." I leaned out the door at him.

"Anytime. Goodnight, Traci."

"Goodnight, Jake."

I watched him drive away towards the interstate and then shut and locked my motel room door. I went back to being single in west Texas.

Bullshit and Beer

09.26.14

The sound of the Indian women making another curry based dish woke me up at 7 a.m. An Indian family owned the Budget Inn. Their kitchen seemed like it was in my bed as her drill-like mixer jarred me awake. I rolled over when the mixer stopped. Screaming babies and a jumble of Punjab music pushed me out of the motel bed. The phone interview for my future job was at 8 a.m., so there was no use staying in bed.

I splashed cold water on my face, smiling in the bathroom mirror. Today was the day! Phone interview for the cool outdoorsy job in Utah and also the first day of the Trans Pecos Festival of Music and Love in Marfa. All that stood between me and three days of love and music was the interview and a quick sixty-mile drive down to Marfa.

I am an expert job getter. There is a rather straightforward formula I follow. Research company. Include words of the mission/vision of the company in my cover letter. Write a relevant resume. Kick ass in the interview by asking questions that are very specific to that company. Get job. Kick ass in said job. I have found the rogue ingredient for kicking ass in a job—and in life—is present moment awareness.

Be mindful. Be awesome. Get any job you desire. Rock that shit 'til the cows come home.

I killed it in the phone interview. Plain and simple. Not because I am a kiss-ass, but because I am a present person who intentionally goes after what I know I want. Ben, the interviewer, was thorough and fun. We talked about my desire to grow and develop as an outdoor educator and he offered information about professional development courses in relevant areas like EMT training opportunities. I was over the moon, walking around the carpeted room as we spoke.

"Oh, one last question," Ben said. "I know you come highly recommended by Todd, but how do you know our Logistics Director

Lauren? She called me right away when your resume came through the ranks."

Lauren is the Logistics Director for Compass Wilderness. She inspects the ropes, helmets, and all the outdoor gear making sure it is safe for the field. Lauren is also someone I went to high school with. She was a freshman when I was the senior captain of our varsity soccer team. She was a hot-shot freshman who played the ball like Nemar when he wasn't broken in Brazil. I remember roughing her up a bit on the field, the way you do to someone you love, someone you see lots of potential in but they are a bit nervous. *That's* how I knew Lauren. I used to be her boss. Now she might become mine.

"Well soccer or otherwise, she burst into my office and told me I needed to hire you. You have a lot of fans from all over," Ben said affirmatively.

I laughed, and felt grateful for my fans. Ben answered a few more of my questions and then he wrapped up the conversation.

"Okay Traci, well if that is all of your questions, we can call this a day!" His tone was that of an enthusiastic surfer. He continued, "The next thing that will happen is, if we decide to move forward, the company will invite you to attend a tryout—eight days of backcountry adventure, simulating what a student would do. This will include rock climbing, rappelling, fire building, and camping. It is a lot of fun. I will be in touch with the decision soon," Ben said.

"Thank you so much, Ben!" I smiled and hung up the phone.

Stoked, nervous, and in disbelief, I packed up my Fort Stockton headquarters into my forty-five-liter backpack. Is Utah really where I am meant to be next? Could this actually be unfolding exactly as I'd wanted? I survived sinking the Titanic and the Carpathia is finally showing up to rescue me and plant me on the solid ground of renewal? *Maybe. Only time will tell.*

I tossed the magnetic key card on the hotel's front desk. Nobody was there but I could smell the curry. I bought an eighty-five-cent cup of coffee at Shell before leaving town. I didn't know eighty-five-cent coffees still existed. It tasted faintly like the artificial hazelnut creamer I used, intermixed with Styrofoam. I cranked one of my CDs on and bombed down I-67, through Alpine, a small town with a University of Texas satellite campus, and further on to Marfa.

Marfa suddenly appeared, like a desert oasis, only it was beginning to rain. Marfa itself was extremely small; I turned down Highland Avenue and the signs for El Cosmico, the festival venue, came up fast. I parked the Chevy in the wet dirt lot, and it began to pour. The first rain I had seen on the desert leg of this trip.

It rained all day. I happily checked in under a white tent and got excited when the volunteer gave me my first ever festival swag: a navy blue Shiner bandana and yellow metal aviators. I meandered into El Cosmico's lobby and admired the souvenirs. They were amazingly hip, cool, and insanely expensive. Shirts, allegedly made from the most organic cotton on the planet, designed with the old Pepsi logo with the word "peyote" replacing Pepsi, sold for a mere $43.50.

This was my first ever camping festival. I had been to all of the music festivals that haunt New Orleans each year, but never to one that you camp out at. I was excited to be dirty, to camp, to sway to music at night with friends I might meet, and maybe even try some drugs.

I held up one of the expensive Peyote shirts to my chest and elbowed a lady next to me.

"Oh! I'm sorry!" I said, turning to face her. I had actually elbowed the woman's adorable brown Chihuahua who was cradled in her right arm. "Is he okay?" I said, feeling foolish. The first encounter with a potential festival friend and I socked her sweet, shivering dog.

"Oh yeah, he is fine, don't worry about it. I'm Sandy, this is Kruze," she said, glancing down at her little dog.

"I love his little flannel dog sweater!" I said, regarding Kruze and Sandy's immaculate appearance. Sandy's golden hair lay straight against her clean Patagonia puff jacket. Her brown heeled boots came up to her knees, so clean I wondered if it was truly raining outside.

She laughed, "Yeah, he is really cold, it is so rainy today."

Another woman, a super-skinny brunette appeared next to Sandy, rubbing Kruze's head.

"This is my sister-in-law, Cathy," Sandy said. Cathy smiled and extended her hand to meet mine.

"Nice to meet you both. I'm Traci."

"My husband, Chris, is outside pitching our tent," Cathy motioned to the lobby's window.

"Where are you guys coming from?" I asked.

"Austin, all three of us," Sandy said. I knew their fashionable festival attire looked familiar.

"Where are you from Traci?"

"New Orleans," I said with a pride I had not felt in a while. I watched their eyes grow wide in reaction.

"Oh wow. Awesome. My husband loves to take trips there for the music festivals, you'll definitely have to find us later for drinks," Cathy said with sudden exuberance.

"Absolutely," I waved to them as they exited the lobby and back into the rain. My first festival friends.

In between rainstorms I pitched my tent like I had been doing it for years, or at least four days in Big Bend. I heard a tiny bark and looked up from the tent stake I was pushing into the ground. It was Kruze. I ended up choosing the grass space next to my new fashionable Austin neighbors.

The forecast called for rain all day in Marfa. The skies were heavy and the cold air was damp. I decided to have a victory beer; for the successful interview and another solid tent pitching moment. I sloshed through the muddy path over to the bar on the side of the lobby. The main bar was not open yet, as the festival still had not officially started. Not until 5 p.m. The side bar consisted of a single, thick cypress wood plank. I ordered a beer and a Topo Chico. Topo Chico is apparently mineral water that's popular in west Texas. I had never ordered it, so it came out mispronounced and with sheepish uncertainty.

A voice behind me laughed and said, "Someone's not from Texas!"

I turned and this gorgeous, clearly Hispanic girl was standing next to me at the wooden plank bar smiling. She was full figured and had a genuine energy that I sensed immediately.

"It is mineral water, and you say it like *toe-po-chee-co*," She enunciated it and the chubby bartender cracked up.

"She's from New Orleans," the bartender said, giving me away. He had carded me moments before.

"Oh cool! I want to visit there. My name is Maria, what's yours, NOLA girl?" She too wore adorable flannel. Just like the Chihuahua. Flannel must be having a moment.

"Traci," I replied.

We got to talking, knocked our beers together in the rain and became fast festivals friends. Maria is 25, though she carries herself with a mature air. She manages a very swanky, kitschy coffeehouse in San Antonio. She was born and raised there under over-protective Mexican-American parents. She had taken a four-day weekend to get out of the busy throes of her city to pitch a tent, rest, and listen to cool music. The rain subsided long enough that we went over to her chosen patch of grass to pitch her blue tent. Maria was floored and inspired when I finally divulged my current state of affairs.

"So you just packed up and left? They really did nothing about the harassment?" She looked up periodically from her tent poles to listen to the story. She wanted to pitch the tent herself, so I stood there watching and answering her questions.

"Yeah, and yeah. I mean as far as I know. HR keeps emailing me back saying they are keeping all actions and resolutions confidential," I said, smearing the mud and gravel mixture at my feet around in little designs.

"That's bullshit. I've just met you, but I can tell you are sweet and amazing. Why do people stay stuck in bullshit ways of operating?" Maria whipped her braided hair behind her shoulder as she rose to her feet, looking at me for an answer.

Oh dear Maria. If I only knew the answer, I wouldn't be sitting here in my tent slamming these keys in catharsis. But, maybe I do know. Or I have at least an inkling.

Q: Why do people stay in bullshit ways of operating?

A: Short answer: fear.

A: Long answer: fear.

Bullshit is safe. Bullshit is how your mother dealt with the abuse, or how your father justified not going for the promotion.

"We have it good, real good, why risk it?" says the nervous father.

Why risk it?

Because your life, your capacity to be fully human depends on you jumping off the cliff of bullshit. Depending on what you believe, you might return to planet earth. Perhaps as a kitten, or an eagle or maybe even an inanimate object. You will be able to participate again. You will lap up milk, soar around, or be a stuffed animal. But this whole human-on-an-overpopulated-overstimulated-oversexed-planet thing? You get one shot. Being on the planet as a human, capable of calling yourself out on bullshit using logic and ballsy reason, is a one-time affair. People stay in the bullshit because it is safer than risk. We come from a lineage of bullshitters, with a few wayfarers, like MLK and Da Vinci, who moved humanity a little bit further by taking risks. The pattern of bullshit stops when you unlearn it. Unfortunately, there is no college course or donation-based workshop on bullshit evolution. You must choose to do the inner work.

I figured the long answer was a bit much for a cool chick I had just met, so I just said, "I don't know Maria, but I am moving forward and getting unstuck," and drank my beer.

She smiled and I retired to my tent for an afternoon nap. We agreed to meet up for the music later.

I slept the afternoon away in the tent; the rain was like a guided meditation as it tapped against the rainfly. I woke up when the kick drum on the music stage was being sound checked. I laid listening to them tune up the electric guitars and microphones. I read, took selfies, and basked in my own safe space. It was the most fun, most uneventful afternoon ever in my tent.

When I left the tent for dinner, the sky was giving off a cool blue as the rainclouds retreated. I ate a glorious falafel sandwich from a vintage food truck. I stood in a half circle with my neighbors, the ones with the stylish Chihuahua, in front of the stage, sharing a bucket of beers. The first band was a 7-piece band called Mother Falcon. I rode their sound for all it was worth—up the violin's pensive spine and down the percussions explosion. I love music. I write music. It felt so good to listen. The moment they pulled out a horn and played it, New Orleans flooded my system. Liquid emotions and memories came up. It brought me back to the first time I heard a horn's sultry sound echoing down Decatur Street in the thick August night. A sound that meant home.

Home, home, home.

Where is home? What does it mean to be there? Is it a state of being or a physical place? Will I ever know when I am home? I didn't know the answer right away so I swayed with all the other Austin hipsters and felt grateful to have made it to the Trans Pecos Festival of Music and Love 2014.

Later I found Maria; she was volunteering her evening at the merchandise booth to pay for her festival ticket. The mini white lights around the wooden booth made her tanned skin appear very soft.

"Let's get together tomorrow, girl," Maria said. She flicked through a rack of t-shirts for a guy standing nearby.

"Sounds good," I replied, and walked back towards the music.

Around midnight, after indulging in five amazing indie bands and endless Shiners, I found my tent in the darkness of the festival grounds. I rummaged through my survival kit and found my headlamp. I brushed my teeth outside and looked up at the stars. It was so tranquil to be outside. I knelt into my tent, traded my bare feet for wool socks and zipped myself into my down sleeping bag.

I was home inside that sleeping bag in Marfa. Home felt cozy, warm, and only two layers of rip stop nylon away from the stardust we are made of. So close to the Maker, so far from the bullshit.

"Thank you," I said as my night prayer.

Prairie Man and Glamping

09.26.14

"Scout, Scout!" A woman's elevated whisper pierced the silent morning. "*Scout*, get over here!" she continued to whisper-yell. I heard Scout sniffing my tent, and then it sounded like he peed on a nearby bush and ran off.

I prepared oatmeal over my camp stove and the hung-over Austinites watched me as if I were a sorcerer. To be concocting that much maple and brown sugar magic that early in the morning was just...*absurd*. They all staggered past me over to the Jo's Coffee tent to purchase $6 breakfast tacos and coffee.

I finished my oatmeal, and wanting to bask in a "real" place, I walked over to Jo's to drink my instant coffee. The coffee shop was actually a 20-foot long open air tent—a burlap army-green tent setup with Jo's coffee, baristas, and chalkboard menus. Two girls, about my age I guessed, walked into the coffeehouse. Miranda and Jenna. I was in the middle of eating an apple with my trail knife, so far removed from my glamping counterparts, when I noticed Jenna eyeing the apple. She was looking at it like a savage, hungry woman.

"Where did you get that apple?" Jenna said, mesmerized, she stepped out of line, inching closer to the apple.

"I packed it in, I had leftover groceries from camping in Big Bend a few days ago," I replied, not sure if the knife would need to become a weapon against this hungry blonde. Her eyeballs got smaller and she smiled wide when I said Big Bend.

"We just got back from Big Bend, too! Sorry, I am feeling so ravenous, we just got here at, like, 3 a.m., driving from Big Bend," she said, pushing her hands against her chest. "We did the backcountry loop to Emory Peak and camped in the Chisos," she continued. I offered them the empty seats across the table from me and they obliged.

"I camped in the Chisos!" I exclaimed. I was thrilled. I had friends.

Cool new friends who run coffeehouses in San Antonio and hike hardcore backcountry routes near Mexico. *Fuck yeah.*

After a long, fun conversation, we realized that the three of us had been trailing the other since Big Bend. The only difference in our itineraries was that they didn't backtrack to Fort Stockton for a date and a job interview.

"Yeah, the boat ride over the Rio Grande to the border town was wild! Did you do it?" Miranda asked eagerly. I thought of Jake, on our date in Fort Stockton, teasing me about not venturing to the border after the Chevy had a hiccup.

"No, I had car trouble," I felt my face blush. They were so much more badass than I was. But now I was badass by association.

I spent the middle part of the day walking around Marfa itself. Marfa is a surreal town, in the middle of nowhere. On the main street, people sat outside their shops petting the ears of mangy dogs that walked by. A couple did acro-yoga on the sidewalk, while a Mexican man in a cowboy hat sold red chilies on a stand in front of the only gas station. Where else do all of these peculiar elements co-exist? I walked all over town, which wasn't very far, and ate lunch at a taco joint. It was a local spot, with stained ceiling tiles, and everyone knew each other except me. I was the only person not wearing cowboy boots and talking about the Marfa Lions football game that night.

It was in the Marfa bookstore where I met Scott and Trent. I ran my hand along the cover of *Death in Big Bend*. I recognized the title as the book the park ranger had raved about in a deranged manner the night I was alone in Big Bend. Suddenly a large hand was on top of mine, both hands on the same book.

"Oh, ah, sorry. My bad…" a good-looking guy said, lifting his hand quickly. "I heard this was a good book…I want to go there," he continued, trying to justify why one might want to grasp for such a morbid title.

"Ah, yeah, I heard it was good too. I just went there and a ranger told me to look it up," I replied, trying not to make things even more awkward.

Was he trying to hit on me? We stood next to the copies of *Death in Big Bend* trying to act like normal individuals who were not truly all that interested in death. Trent, Scott's buddy, walked in the store briskly, rescuing us both from our foolishness.

"Uh guys, there's a gnarly storm coming this way, are you heading back to the festival, too?" Trent said, looking at Scott first, and then to me questioningly. He was a scruffy looking guy with a face that held equal parts tan and dirt. I shook my head yes.

Trent held out his hand, "I'm Trent and this is Scott."

"I'm Traci," I shook Scott's hand properly after Trent's. Together the three of us raced out the door without purchasing a copy of *Death in Big Bend*.

The gnarly swirling cloud of darkness about to pummel the festival campground looked like Death in Marfa. We hauled ass on foot back to camp, during which time I told them the synopsis of what brought me to Marfa, between labored breaths of speed-walking: that I was on a road trip to nowhere, following the muse and she had taken me to a funky, folky music festival in the heart of west Texas where hipsters converged. I said there was "trouble" at work, feeling afraid to share the whole truth with two guys I'd just encountered. As we walked I noticed how tan, muscular, and fucking sexy Scott was. He had a full, reddish beard and wavy golden hair.

"Yah, we drove here from Missouri. We both work on the same CSA farm," Trent said, while I discreetly evaluated Scott's chiseled arms as he strode in front of us. They were true good ol' boys from the South, with good hearts.

We made it to the back gate and found Maria there to let us in; she was doing her second and final volunteer stint. She let us in, I introduced my new festival friends, and we would later become a little tribe making rogue expeditions into Marfa for the next forty-eight hours.

"He is really *cute*." Maria put an extra emphasis on the word cute and motioned to Scott in the distance.

"I know," I giggled, making big enunciations with my lips. I told her about our awkward meeting in the bookstore and she held her stomach in laughter. We stood inside the back gate watching the dark clouds move across the windy sky, letting people with pink wristbands through the tall metal gate. Five minutes later, Scott tracked back over to the gate.

"Ah, if you'd like to, me and Trent are staying in that gold van over there. You can—I mean you *both* are welcome to come over for a beer later," he stumbled through his words, encompassing both Maria and I in a sweeping hand motion.

"Great. Yeah, that sounds good!" I said, looking into his vivid blue eyes for the first time.

"Yeah, that'd be killer," Maria echoed.

"Sweet. Well, you ladies enjoy the rest of your day," he said and walked away, his cowboy boots kicking up dirt in his wake.

"He's got the body of a Greek god…he's like a prairie man," Maria went on, as he walked off, watching him with her chin cradled in her hand.

"Yeah, his ass looks great in those jeans," I said, enjoying the view as well. His dirty white tank top just added to the appeal of his rugged appearance.

"I'd grab a hold of him and don't let go, girlfriend!" Maria insisted, squeezing my shoulder playfully. She said something in Spanish under her breath snapping her fingers back and forth, pretending to fan herself.

Mmmm, I love me a rugged man with facial hair. Only dated one in cowboy boots, and the sex was hot.

After Maria's shift of guarding the gate was complete, and the apocalyptic storms had blown over, we went to the guys' van to have a beer. It was around 4 p.m. and the sound check was starting again with the kick drum. Maria and I crept up on the van through the tall yellow grass.

"Hey, you two!" she said warmly.

"Hello there, ladies," Trent said, opening a beat-up Igloo cooler and handing us both icy cold Modelos.

Scott cleared a little spot off the back of the van's open back doors and offered the space. There was sage burning inside the van in a nearby cup holder and books about spirituality and chakras were piled on a homemade shelf. Maria and I sat down together on the edge of the van with our beers. Trent was sitting in a chair, chewing a piece of grass in his mouth, and Scott sat on what looked to be an empty wooden dresser drawer. After some initial banter it was revealed that the van was Scott's; he bought it in California on a whim, fixed it up, and drove back to Missouri, where his mother was. That is where he began work on the CSA farm, and met Trent.

The conversations eventually turned one-on-one, and Trent took one for the team. Modelo after Modelo, he angled Scott and I at each other, more directly each time.

A few hours had passed and Scott and I were knee-deep in the ideas of buying land, what it would take to build a tiny home, and create a sustainable community. I was enthralled with him and stunned to meet a man with similar, intuitively-guided goals.

"So where would you buy land?" he asked me, also chewing on a piece of straw.

"Right now, I'm not sure, since my life is so up in the air, but I know I want the four seasons," I responded.

"Ah me too! There is something so grounding about each season," he said, his voice was quiet and contemplative. He inhaled a deep breath and looked off into the distance for a moment before turning back at me. "Do you like gardening? I would love to have a garden on my land."

"Oh yeah I would for sure, but I'm not very good at it," I said, hoping my lack of a green-thumb wasn't an automatic disqualification for our future marriage.

"I could show you a thing or two," he said quietly, looking deeply into my eyes.

God, he is hot. Not just because of his tan, or the fact that he is adventurous and living in a van, or his amazing ass. I found him incredibly attractive due to his genuine personality. He listens. He speaks about what he is passionate about, with vigor and happiness.

The sun set in the cleared sky as we sat at the back of a gold van. At a festival. In Marfa, Texas. Four people who had just met. Just chasing life the best way we knew how—without wearing fancy cowgirl or cowboy hats.

On day two of any event you tend to get a better lay of the land. When I ventured around after the sunset more folks had arrived, having waited out the rain. The Trans Pecos festival was amazingly weird; a temporary Austin infused Los Angeles mini-world occupied the eighteen acres of El Cosmico. The vendors consisted of hipsters clad in thick black glasses selling "vintage" clothing out of renovated airstreams. The vintage clothing was stuff they wore, or their parents wore in 1987, and they sold each item for a cool $32 or so. Totally weird, and totally genius. My eveningwear came straight from my car's trunk and I ran the risk of not looking the part.

The music started at twilight, the crowd gathered, looking like they all had stepped out of a Wrangler meets Armani ad in the desert. The ladies wore pristine cowgirl boots, overpriced jeans, leather hats and pretty flannel shirts with cute turquoise jewelry. Some men wore skinny jeans, boots, and army green shirts with retro national park patches sewn on. Other guys sported plaid shirts with bolero ties and the obligatory ranch-hand hat. Everyone kept their shades on as the sun set across from the stage. I felt underdressed, and in awe of how everyone had a signal on their iPhones. I had on dirty hiking boots that needed gorilla glue, and my cell hadn't had a signal since Fort Stockton.

Also, more Chihuahuas showed up. It was like two hundred Paris Hilton-wannabes heard about a festival two hours from the Mexican border. Some dogs walked with their owners wearing booties to protect from muddy paws. Other Chihuahuas rode in the space between their owner's boobs and puff jacket zipper.

"I don't get it…" I said to Miranda and Jenna, my mouth ajar. We stood on the fringe of the crowd and watched the well dressed women who came out of the giant white tents far off from the stage.

"They're glamping," Jenna said matter-of-factly.

"What is *glamping*?" I asked.

"Glamorous camping, glamping," Jenna said, offering me a cup of red wine. "Those big white tents cost $600 a night. They have beds, rugs, electricity, all of the normal life amenities, but in a tent," she said.

"Wow, I didn't even know that was a thing," I said. The most glamorous I had gotten so far was shaving my legs at the Budget Inn.

Life is so weird, and interesting. What are all these people about? Why are they here? *I am a refugee from New Orleans, what could their story be?*

Dinnertime came, and I feasted at a different food truck. The night was cold, so I relished in the warmth of a hot chocolate from Jo's coffeehouse. Miranda, Jenna, and I rocked out to some rock band, talking about the day in between songs. It sounded like almost all of us ventured into town today.

Maria had disappeared to help another friend setup his tent who had just arrived to town. I spotted Scott and Trent across the crowd. I waved in their direction and Scott came over quickly. He was wearing the jean jacket he had offered to me earlier at the van when the cold front finally pushed through town. Jenna and Miranda left to get more wine from the main bar, leaving Scott and I alone in the center of the smartly-dressed crowd.

"Look up," he said. The clarity of the western stars was mesmerizing. We both stood there, staring up above the stage lights. I felt warm...more like hot, next to him. I wanted to be so close to Scott, not just because it was cold and I could see my breath in the desert air, but because I felt like we knew each other. Similar to Jake. Like this is how it had always been; we always went to festivals together. I wanted him to hold me. To hug me. He gave off such a comforting energy.

He leaned his head down close to my ear and said, "I just wanted to say that based on what you were talking of earlier, I like what you are bringing into the world, all the positive stuff. You are doing big things and I want to know all about it. I think you are a beautiful woman."

I leaned up to his ear on my tiptoes, "Thank you," I said over the music. There was so much I wanted to say to him. "Do you believe that we are all connected, like, on a universal level?" I asked.

"Yes absolutely, and we are constantly teaching each other lessons," he replied without hesitation. His breath was warm in my ear.

"Can we stay in touch? I'd love that," he asked.

We exchanged numbers. I pictured him on a tractor on our land, with the tiny home we had built together in the background. *Our little children running around barefoot.*

"Well I'm gonna go wind down. You're welcome to come by the van…" he said. It was past midnight and the band was starting to come down a notch. I politely declined and he gave me a strong, manly hug goodnight.

Mmmm. Hold me just a little longer, prairie man.

Real Men Cry
09.27.14

It is day three of the Trans Pecos Festival. I feel as though I've been here for ages. It is that feeling on any journey when the traveler sinks into the feeling of "here" and "place." I was home, at least temporarily, in my tent in Marfa. I made my instant coffee and oatmeal on the camp stove, watching the tribes of free spirited children roam the rapidly warming festival grounds. There were about ten of them, a mixture of boys and girls about ages seven to eleven. They walked around like a gang; a pack of already expressive hippie humans in touch with their sense of self. One girl wore only a glittery leotard and red rain boots complimented by sweet blonde pigtails.

Why? Why the hell not? Because she is seven and societal norms have not hit her with left hooks to the kidneys. No kid in that group had gotten into a fist fight yet with normal society as far as I could see. The norms that dictate what we must wear, that it must match, that we can't twirl around in the grass and dance in self-expression. By the looks of their parents, who were the very definition of the vagabond hippie, these kids might have the potential to rewrite the societal norms through their lifestyle choices. The parents watched and laughed as their mini-hippies created a game from sticks and a tire.

I watched from the open door of my orange and gray tent, transfixed by the wisdom found in the festival kids. To be open, to laugh, to do whatever you are moved to do…including dance in red rain boots wearing only a glittery leotard because it makes your insides feel good.

I went inside El Cosmico's lobby in a slight transcendent haze from the children's energy buzz. I set up my computer at a long wooden table and sank into adulthood. Today being the last day of the festival, I needed to again do some traveler house-cleaning. The usual suspects were on my written to-do list: emails, credit card payment, and securing a place to rest my head at my next destination.

My inbox was filled with emails from Compass Wilderness. My heart jumped in happiness. I read the first one; they were impressed with my interview and skills and wanted to formally invite me to Utah for the guide tryout! I was thrilled, nervous, and amazed at how fast life can accelerate when you just ask for what you want. Truly be careful, because it *will* become your reality.

Suddenly I needed to make plans to get to Utah in seven days, to participate in the job tryout of a lifetime; to live in the backcountry for eight days doing all sorts of outdoor badass stuff that hopefully, if I aced the course, I would be running with students who are in need of wilderness therapy. I sent a few hopeful couchsurfing requests for Santa Fe and smiled at the computer. I am going to Utah in a week to do a week of adventure! Holy shit!

In the afternoon Maria and I went to an annual baseball game that the festival put on. It was between a bunch of guys called the "Austin Playboys" and the "Marfa Cocks". We arrived to the sandlot field across town at around one o'clock. The sun was hot and high above us. A crew of Marfa locals and festival workers dressed up in all sorts of costumes lined the third base fence. Three women with pink tutus and wigs danced on the dugout shouting, "Go cocks!" The announcers were two local guys who ran the public radio station. They were about four tall boys in, taunting the caged rooster that was in the wooden press box with them. It seemed the whole festival and town of Marfa was there, everyone about four beers in, except for Maria and I.

Scott and Trent flagged us down with a friendly wave. They had saved room for us on the peeling green bleachers. It was like watching the grown-up version of the Sandlot narrated by Dane Cook. Inappropriate jokes about each player's baseball pants rang out into the stands, cock references never ceased, and everyone kept getting increasingly drunk. The game was wildly entertaining; a hippie child dressed in a rooster costume that flopped around over his tiny body ran in front of the bleachers incessantly yelling "go cocks!" Collective laughter permeated the bleachers. Beach balls bounced through the crowd. So good. So right. So strangely correct to be drinking a tall can of Dos Equis and noshing on a hot dog while watching a bad baseball game with crude announcers. At some point Trent spontaneously got up and motioned for Scott and me to smile for a picture. Scott's hand gripped my hips strongly and he pulled me close. His beard was rough against my cheek. I flushed with happiness and got turned on by his surprise force.

I never did get that photo. Maybe Trent will print it out for the wedding reception.

The hippie children and their parents did the halftime dance show and nobody questioned that we were calling it a halftime show for a baseball game. Around 3 p.m., most of the people retreated back to the festival grounds to shower and put on their fancy cowboy boots for one more night of prancing and music. The four of us stuck around until the announcers couldn't remember if the halftime show had already occurred and started slurring the names of the players at bat. The game ended abruptly at inning thirteen, but we couldn't be sure if it was actually only the bottom of the ninth. The Playboys and the Cocks shook hands and the Playboys took the win eleven to eight.

I washed up in the portable showers on a trailer when I got back. The sun was getting hazy behind some fluffy white clouds and a cool breeze chilled my wet skin as I walked back to my tent in a towel. I changed into warmer clothes for the night's music and went over to the boys' gold van. I was hoping to steal a moment with Scott. To ambush him at the van. I hadn't really planned the ambush. I wasn't sure if I would push him down onto the floor of the van and kiss him deeply, or ask him to talk about the chakra system over tea.

Neither fantasy happened. Instead Trent was there, setting up a game of solitaire.

"Hey! Where's your other half?" I said, trying to mask my disappointment for encountering Trent alone at the van and not my prairie man.

Trent walked me to the front of the van, where a dirt road encircled the entire property. He pointed down the road and said, "Wait here."

I waited, wondering what in the world Scott was up to. The sound of a motorcycle engine ripped through the quiet waning afternoon. A cloud of dust surrounded Scott as he raced up the road coming at me on a red 1970's Honda two-stroke. His hair moved in the wind dramatically and his gold aviators reflected the setting sun.

Goddddd, take me now.

He revved the engine as he stopped the bike at my feet. He smiled devilishly and I bit my lower lip instinctively.

"Isn't this awesome?" He yelled over the engine. "One of the guys picked up this bike on the way down from Colorado for $600. I'd been begging him to let me take it for a spin!" He was beaming with happiness.

The fog of his hotness lifted for long enough that I glimpsed myself in him. That unabated joy I tap into when I am living super fucking hard, doing anything and everything that moves me, day by day. I recalled the hippie children dancing in the field this morning with the sticks and glittery leotards. Scott, as far as I could tell, had managed to evolve into a man, albeit a restless wandering man, without the proverbial Man telling him how to live a "normal" life. Scott was the adult version of the kids this morning, minus the glittery leotard and pigtails. His vigor for life gave me a surge of inspiration.

"It is *so* cool! Looks like you are having a blast!" I said, wanting him to toss me on the back and drive us out of town without anything but the clothes on our back. But he was a little too busy with his inner child for that.

"I'm gonna take one more lap, catch you guys in a bit!" He raced off, leaving me with Trent and solitary solitaire.

"Do you want to go for a walk?" Trent asked.

"Sure," I said, and we followed Scott's dust trail up the road.

"...So, the other day, when we walked back here from the bookstore, you mentioned you left New Orleans because of crap at work. What happened to make you get in your car and drive so far away?" he asked, his brown eyes were so earnest. So ready to listen.

So I recounted the whole story. Just as I had done with Maria, Heather, and Christina, and countless other people who now held a piece of my New Orleans departure story like a puzzle piece. Trent, however, was the first grown man I had told the whole story to. The first man who witnessed me rage openly about other men who he had never met. It felt weird, it felt mean, but I felt honest and relieved. I said the words, "sexual" and "harassment" to a man, feeling a sense of shame, wondering whether or not he would believe the whole story and whether or not he would respect it.

The gravel stopped crunching under his boots abruptly. He stopped walking and cried. I was already crying, and two lonely tears came down his left cheek. Then many, many, tears slid down through his whiskered face. He opened his arms, inviting me into his embrace. I clawed at his dirty white t-shirt like a crazed, scared animal. He hugged me hard, big brother style, and I cried harder, shaking with release. He just held me. This was the hold of love I had been craving for what seemed like an eternity.

What kind of man cries for a strange woman's plight in the middle of nowhere? A caring man, that's who. Not some prick from New Orleans who doesn't give a fuck. A real man cries. He recognizes that he is made in the image of God and that his being is both divine masculine and divine feminine. Real men evolve into better contributors to this lovely world when they realize this balance. When they recall those hippie kid days spent at festivals laughing, crying, even wearing glittery leotards, if that's what moved them.

At some point the fight with society and it's fucked up norms happened and our boys were ruthlessly educated about what a true man is. They learned from billboards that real men wear expensive suits, have gorgeous, skinny—and most likely highly-disempowered—women hang on them, and their masculinity orbits their balls. Being a man morphed into outdated clichés of "winning bread" and "not showing emotion".

As women, we are taught that we need our men strong.

Baby, let me tell you something. I thought for a very long time that what would complement my womanliness was a strong man who didn't cry. He would powerfully seduce me with a martini at the top of the Manhattan skyline while I wore a little black dress. I thought this, and I manifested it. This was my life. I almost married the man who bought me those martinis and held back his tears. But thankfully I listened to my divine inner goddess and realized I wanted balance more than the great sex I was promised by billboard ads.

Real men do ride motorcycles and burp. They jack off. They are gross. But they also allow themselves to feel through life.

"Nobody should have to go through that," Trent sniffed back some tears, "I'm sorry, it just makes me so upset, my sister had something similar happen..." his voice cracked and trailed off.

"You're right, nobody should have to encounter that, man or woman," I said, rubbing his back.

"Even if I didn't have a sister. Why are people so cruel to each other? You are amazing and I can sense how strong you are." Trent grabbed both of my shoulders and stared into my eyes. "People who are filled with light scare other people who haven't realized their light yet. They want to stamp you out because they don't know how to light their own candle. Please don't stop being you, Trace," he continued, his eyes still two glass panels.

Trent's honesty poured out. His level of self-awareness was high. He floored me with the reference to inner light. I didn't know some men are on the vibration of love and light. That some men are truly awakening and realizing that having a penis is only one piece to a very complex external and internal make up. Trent made me hopeful. Good men, good people, who love and seek to be loved, are all around us.

That night there wasn't a huge fireworks display or any other form of a dramatic climax to signal the end of the festival. However, there was a final night of great music, grilled cheese, staggering stars, and friends. An air of love swept around me. All the hugs, the laughs, the purity that encircled me in the last three days. It was all love.

Love. Love. Love.

The Trans Pecos Festival of Music and Love, 2014.

She Works Hard for the Money
09.28.14

There comes the end to every festival of music and love. I awoke to people hugging, taking selfies, and rushing around breaking their camps before the morning dew had even a hope of drying. Alas, it was Sunday and the real world was beckoning the members of said real world back into its evil grasp.

By the time I rolled out of my pup tent, all the glampers and their pint-sized Chihuahuas had already peeled out onto Route 90, presumably headed back to their warm showers and cozy beds in Austin or LA.

As for me—well, I didn't have anywhere in particular to be in the fabled real world. I had tentatively lined up some work helping to break down the festival with Trent, but we had made the deal in drunken stupor, so today I needed to do some legwork. I've always wanted to work at a festival or some sort of gig at least once in my life.

Today was the day my dream of being a quasi-carnie came true. At breakfast the scene was humorous and bittersweet; hung over festival goers wearing Ray Bans cried into their Bloody Marys as we all said our goodbyes to each other. Maria and I took a photo together and vowed to stay in touch. Scott caught my eye as he sauntered over from the breakfast line, his plate full of pancakes and fresh fruit.

He sat down next to me, nudging into my shoulder sweetly. "Morning you two," he said.

Maria held up her pink iPhone at us. "Alright you two, photo time," she snapped the picture and I transmitted a girl-coded thank-you with my eyes.

We all devoured the breakfast; it was such a welcome treat after so many oatmeal mornings.

"So, are you still interested in staying over here one more night and working today?" Scott inquired.

"Yeah totally," I said.

He got up and gestured for me to follow him. We walked over to a nearby picnic table and he leaned into a tall bald guy with a full beard and a sun burnt neck.

"Mike, this is Traci, she wants to help today, breaking down the scout tents, do you still need extra hands?" Scott was holding his plate in his hands, now working on the fresh fruit.

Mike shook my hand while balancing a mimosa in the other. "Nice to meet you. Yah, I definitely need help today. Find the yellow Penske truck at noon and we will take it from there. $15 an hour, cash."

"Great" I said, and we all scattered.

I spent the rest of the morning straightening up my tent, hanging out with Maria, and trying to book a place to stay in Santa Fe. That was my next and suddenly final stop before driving to the job tryout in Utah. All morning I forcefully tried to reign in my otherwise spontaneous trip, and failed miserably. My Airbnb account wouldn't work, and no couchsurfing request were coming through. I was still stoked on the prospect of being out in the wilderness in one short week, but a sense of foreboding floated around me. *Why the sudden resistance? Where is the magic? Is it departing with the Austin hipsters? Maybe I am not meant to go to Santa Fe. Of course I am, my vision board in my storage unit says so.* I shut my computer at 11:45, hugged Maria; she wished me luck in the upcoming tryout, and we parted ways.

I found Mike around 12:15 at his gigantic Penske truck. There were only three other people that wanted to work all afternoon for some fast cash. It seemed like a no brainer; all we needed to do was drop the tents. Granted they were larger shelter tents, but it didn't look that intimidating.

Nothing is ever as it seems.

There were thirty-three tents. Thirty-three tents that the glampers paid $600 per night to stay in. Jenna and Miranda's description of the tents came to life when I opened the door to tent number one, and gasped at all of the furniture inside. A queen Ikea mattress was in the back center of the tent with a down comforter and earth toned throw pillows. Two wooden nightstands with battery lamps flanked the bed, while two leather chairs and ottomans stood at a face off near the tent entrance. A small cow hide accent rug was covered in empty beer bottles on the floor and the tent smelled like sex. I looked around the tent ruefully. I had no idea all of that was inside *each* tent. Glamping was serious. It's a serious money-maker, and it ended up being a serious pain in my delirious ass seven hours later.

I love to work hard and use my body. I love to sweat. To bend, to lift, to push and pull. To feel the strength of my body as I move heavy objects. However, as we entered hour three, and the only other guy peeled off Operation Take Down the Glamp Camp, I started to waver in my desire to work hard for cold cash. The cow rugs pricked my arms with stray pieces of sharp grass as I carried them into the van. My hands cracked and bled a little. I thought I was going to die of heat exhaustion as the desert sky poured down sun. What a way to go out, I daydreamed as I carried the throw pillows in a garbage bag to the truck; death from trying to earn some cash by cleaning up glamp camp. *Rich motherfuckers*. I was a mere peasant, a wandering woman trying to earn her road money to tramp north tomorrow. Was it my destiny to die in Marfa after an amazing festival just for gas money?

Thankfully, it wasn't in the cards. We broke for dinner and then Mike, looking very out of it from heat and three days of hard day drinking, called it a day.

"I'm staying over another night, we will finish in the morning," he said, handing me and my two other festival gig working comrades some cold Fat Tire cans of beer. "Good work y'all, I don't know what I woulda done without you," he said, fanning out twenties to each of us.

The cash felt good in my hands. I stashed it away promptly, felt how sunburned my nose had gotten, and retired to the glorious portable on-site showers. I bathed, shaved my legs, and put lotion on my nose. I watched one final epic sunset on the Texas horizon from a two-person hammock that hung between two oak trees. Scott came walking up.

"I heard y'all didn't finish the job," he said from beneath a brown derby hat.

"Yeah, we only had three people. How did tearing down the stage go?" I replied. I sat up in the hammock, happy to see him again.

"It was really hard, but we got it done." His bare arms and face looked extra tan from the day's work.

"If you want, Trent and I are staying in one of the teepees tonight, feel free to come by, otherwise make sure you find me to say goodbye in the morning."

"Okay, I will." I smiled and watched him walk off, again coveting his cute ass in those flattering Levis.

I was too tired to go hang out with my guys so I crashed in my tent early. It stood alone. It was a weird night, solemn and lonely since the other three hundred people had departed throughout the day. It was again me, my tent, and the Texas stars. I decided I'd say goodbye to the boys in the morning, and drifted off into sleep.

Part Five: New Mexico

Fear is a natural reaction to moving closer to the truth.
- Pema Chödrön

TRACI ANN

New Mexico: The Land of...Panic?
09.29.14

The sun shone through the little porthole shaped window on the rainfly of my tent, stirring me awake. My body ached from yesterday's tent dismantling. The tent was soaked with condensation, which meant I couldn't fully pack it away before driving, but I didn't care. I felt alive. It was Monday and I had no set schedule except the exciting job tryout in Utah, seven days from now.

Today I would travel to Santa Fe, New Mexico. The Land of Enchantment. One hour north of Santa Fe, in Taos, was my original ending point on my road trip. In early August I applied and got accepted into the Earthship Academy, a five-week hands-on sustainable building school. The same Friday I resigned from NORP, I deferred my acceptance to the Taos program, knowing it sadly was not a financial option. Still, New Mexico somehow stood as a bookend for my travels.

As I crouched inside the moist tent, packing up my belongings, I suddenly remembered pieces of a terrifying dream I had last night. I dreamt I was clutching my chest, out of breath. A close friend from New Orleans was with me in the dream. She held me up from behind, desperately asking what was wrong.

"I don't know, I just can't catch my breath," I replied with an empty look, hands clutching my chest. The dream floated around in the Marfa atmosphere. I tried to push it out of my psyche. I dream hard and vividly, so I pushed that sucker as far down as possible.

Scott walked up the path, his brown cowboy boots with the rope tied around the right one making lots of noise in the quiet morning.

"Hey! Glad you're still here, I got you some coffee from inside, need a hand with that?" he pointed to the red El Cosmico wagon filled with my backpack, pillow, and teddy bear on the top. My temperature increased. Shit, the teddy bear, I am not the sexy road-trip homebuilder girl anymore. I am the bizarre twenty-eight-year-old wanderer who still sleeps with a raggedy teddy bear. Damn. I took the second coffee from his hands.

"I just travel with the teddy bear," I said nonchalantly.

"It's cute," Scott said. "Here, let me wheel that to your car," he smiled, and we went to my car and packed up my home.

I sipped the coffee and enjoyed being with him. Trent emerged from El Cosmico's lobby, with coffee in his hands as well.

"Good morning, glad we didn't miss sending you off," he wrapped his arms around me and I caught a smell of soap. "You are so strong, Traci, you are an amazing woman, and you are on the path…keep going and trust the process," Trent said, releasing me with a giant exhale.

Scott stepped up for his hug. I wanted to kiss him, like we were always together and this was just a little separate adventure we both had to go on. He dug around in his pockets, producing a rock filled with crystals, and a small bag of seeds tied with delicate rope.

"This is crystal from Arkansas, it has really good energy, keep it close to you. And…these are arugula seeds, for when you build your home. You can plant them in your garden."

We hugged for a long time. And I knew. I knew he was either one of two things, or both: the man I would somehow find in the future and share space with, or a guardian angel that the universe placed on my path to provide loving kindness for me during such a difficult time. Both men, so strong and rugged, yet so respectful, gentle, and the opposite of the guys who had hurt me so badly. How does that exist? Such different people? Does the universe always send you what you need, even if it is painful?

"Well, I guess I'll see you guys later," I said, positioning the crystal in my cup holder and rolling down all the windows. "Thank you for everything, I know we'll cross paths again."

"We sure will," Scott replied. They stood next to each other waving at me as I turned out of the parking lot.

I cruised out of the festival grounds towards Santa Fe on a natural high; wearing my new yellow aviators, my mind marveled at all of the amazing festival moments. I relaxed in the driver's seat, feeling less scared of the wild open road in front of me, yet it was still very solemn, the horizon still brown and endless.

I stopped in El Paso at a crowded, Spanish-speaking McDonalds to eat and finally get through on the Airbnb website to confirm my Santa Fe accommodations. Karen, a prize-winning quilter lady with white hair, had agreed to host me. I got back on the road around 1 p.m., stopped on the shoulder to snap a picture of the New Mexico state line sign and got stabbed in the leg by a prickly pear cactus.

Onward I drove. When I stopped to get gas in a random place called Truth and Circumstance, a sliver of disorientation was registered in my rapidly dehydrating body. I was gaining altitude the whole drive. I had been at altitude before, so I didn't pay it much mind. I bought a blue Gatorade from the lady behind the counter. She handed me my change without looking up from her crossword puzzle.

Around 3:30, my cell got signal again and its GPS system started talking to me. Her voice was a welcome change of pace; the radio hadn't worked since El Paso and I was getting tired of Macklemore telling me about his thrift shop finds.

"Keep straight on I-25 north," she said, in that confident GPS tone. A mileage sign flew at me saying, *Albuquerque: 100 miles.* That meant Santa Fe was only sixty miles from there…mere child's play compared to the driving I had gotten used to. I got this.

During the next two hours, something inside of me started to unravel. Like a ball of yarn that a cat batted down the stairway. My mind began to unfurl. Something triggered thoughts of Steph and I wailed on the steering wheel—pounding on it and searching for clean tissues as I sobbed and drove. I sobbed for our friendship death, for the job I no longer had, for all the pain that oozed through my chakras.

Where is all this coming from? I'm fine, right? I just came from the festival of all festivals, why would I feel shitty now? I tried to reason with my tired, yarn-ball mind.

My heart thumped in my ears rapidly as I navigated through downtown Albuquerque. Something wasn't right in my body. Something told me to stop, to not finish the final sixty miles to Santa Fe where Karen and her guestroom awaited me. It was a deep, urgent cry to stop. I'm so glad we have our intuitive parts. Our internal GPS. If we listen to it, we will always be led down the correct path.

The final exit on Interstate 25 before continuing to Santa Fe came up quick and I veered right onto the ramp. "Recalculating," said the external GPS. I pulled off at the first gas station I saw and got out of the car immediately. Disoriented, agitated as fuck, and scared, I staggered around the gas station like a drunk. I didn't know what do. Why could I not inhale a full breath? My body begged for more oxygen and my heart was pounding. I used my final ounces of clear thinking and stumbled over to a man in a suit, fueling his blue hatchback.

"Hi… I'm Traci. I think I'm having an anxiety attack or altitude sickness," I wheezed out slowly, trying not to alarm him or myself. "I need you to take me to the hospital or call an ambulance." I stared at him in terror.

His face went from shock and alarm to serious and focused. "Okay, right, get your ID and purse and any medication from your car, lock it and come back over here right away," he said, with one hand on his hip and the other pointing me back to my car.

Holy shit. This life.

My hands shook in a violent and foreign way as I searched in the three-tiered shower tower for my medicines. I saw my teddy bear underneath a pile of maps in the backseat and tossed him in my purse before locking the car's doors. I was having my first ever anxiety attack mixed with being at altitude. Miraculously I had pulled off at the exit that contained one of the best medical center in town and found Marc, my ride to the ER.

He walked me into the ER, guiding me by the elbow. A woman seated behind a plexiglass divider motioned for me to sit down.

"What brings you here tonight, my dear?" she asked, fingers poised above her keyboard.

"I think anxiety, or altitude, pain in my chest," I gasped loudly, pressing a hand firmly against my chest, trying to make the pain stop. Awareness punctured me like a bullet in the brain. The dream. The dream of holding my chest this morning.

The rest of the night was a whirlwind. It was like a lucid dream turned nightmare that got fucked hard in the ass while tripping on peyote. Hospital wristband. Pattered hospital gown. Technician rapidly taking blood from me to run it for test results. The IV leaking blood before I got hooked into the saline solution, squirting my blood on the hospital bed. The electronic prongs being hooked up to my chest and legs to monitor my heart, cold chest x-rays to rule out a pulmonary embolism. Was I dying now? And why? It sure as hell seemed like I had a lot more to do on this Earth…including tryout for a killer outdoor job in Utah on Sunday.

I went in and out of sleep in the hospital bed while I waited for the test results to come back. Different combinations of beeping machines and the yells of a hysterical older woman lulled me back and forth between the worlds of sleep and consciousness.

"Sweetie, you are lucky lady!" A nurse in green scrubs whipped back the curtain around the bed. "You just asked a random man at a gas station to bring you to the hospital?" My nurse, Aire, scolded me as I came to.

Like I had a choice. It was either that or stagger around until I passed out near the diesel pumps.

"I didn't know what else to do," I said, so deeply shaken and physically exhausted. I rubbed my palms together; they were no longer clammy.

"Well you just happened to have pulled off on the hospital exit and found yourself a very kind man. This is a very dangerous city," she marked off a few things on her clipboard. "What do you do for exercise?" Aire asked, peering at me from above her glasses.

I was confused. "I work in the outdoors usually, and do yoga," I replied. She shook her head like she already knew this about me.

"You are as healthy as a horse, your blood work is great, and so are your lungs. It looks like you had your first anxiety attack combined with being at altitude. Have you had any recent trauma?"

"Sort of, not really." I did not want to engage.

Recent trauma. Yes. Damn you, body! You wait until now, until a week before a stellar job interview to crash and burn in trauma. *Shit. Shit. Shit. Shit.* I have to deal with this shit. I can't outrun it.

Reality is a cold hard bitch. She is like that scary teacher you despised in high school. Startling you in the middle of the hallway asking, "Are you prepared for the exam?" You fumble around looking for your notes. You left them in the locker, the bell already rang, and it is time for the test. Reality does not wait. She only teaches.

It seems that I signed up for Healing 101 and class started today. But no! That's not part of my plan. I am supposed to work in Utah and be a super rad outdoor girl who has crystals from respectable prairie men, not mental battle scars from sexual perpetrators in the dirty South.

I caught a cab back to the Chevy at 10 p.m. It was truly a miracle, today, all of it. I could have been mugged. The Chevy could have been stolen. I could have crashed my car if I kept going. But it wasn't. It was still there when I returned wearing a hospital wristband. The world is truly filled with kind people, and even in our worst states, we can project our genuine light to attract other light beings. I drove two blocks up the road. The lady at the counter of the Best Western eyed my hospital band suspiciously.

"Do you guys accept Triple A discounts?" I asked, praying for a little more luck to end the evening.

"Yes we do," she said, handing me two key cards. "Breakfast is in the café over there tomorrow from seven to nine." She pointed to a darkened café across the lobby.

"Great, thank you so much."

I crumbled into the incredibly soft bed and hoped for clarity by morning.

TRACI ANN

Expensive Taxi, Panic, and Santa Fe Miracles
09.30.14

It sucks balls when you get sexually harassed at work. It sucks old wrinkly balls when you have your first full blown panic attack while driving at seven thousand feet, most likely due to the trauma of being harassed and abruptly resigning from your job.

"Yes, I feel well enough to drive the sixty miles to Santa Fe," I murmured to my dad over the phone in the Best Western after breakfast.

"Well then, drive the sixty miles, and call me when you get there, okay?" he said in an understanding tone. "I will be at your mother's retirement party, but I can step out, so please call."

"Okay. I love you, dad."

"Love you too Trace."

We got off the phone and I sobbed for a time. Not for anything in particular, but for everything non-particular. For people dying around the world for lame ass reasons we only have false truths for via news media. For being unemployed and wandering. For gratitude at having a dad that is present in my life and calls me to ask if I am healthy. For the crater in my heart that used to house New Orleans.

The sobs carried me to my knees. I got as close to the floor as I possibly could…drawing my knees to my chest and wailed loudly in the hotel room. Desperately trying to purge old shit. Old shit. Old baggage.

Old baggage clings to you like that guy at the bar who is still holding out hope that you'll have sex with him if he keeps buying you cheap tequila shots. Heavy, icky, nasty. When it feels like this my friend, *that* is real motherfucking baggage. Emotionally rooted, physically manifesting, spiritually transformative oversized luggage and TSA is definitely not checking that shit for you. They are going to take one look at it and realize it is yours to carry on. They don't care if the atom bomb is in there…because they already know it is…they just want to get you to Cleveland and off their damn plane. Those of you who openly acknowledge your baggage are seen as horribly scary people to normal society. People who live in neighborhoods with high walled curbs, and edged lawns, they don't want you around. These folks put their oversized emotional trunks in the extra bedroom closet of their McMansion ten years ago. Don't you even *think* about wheeling that sucker around in their neighborhood.

My watch beeped. 11 a.m. I needed to check out of the Best Western. Yes, I was feeling healthy enough to drive, I reasoned with myself. It is only sixty miles. One hour. What could possibly happen in one hour?

The sunshine felt scrumptious on my face as I walked to my car in the parking lot. My hospital wristband was still on, as I hadn't asked anyone for a pair of scissors to cut it off. The Chevy roared to life, and so did I.

"I am driving to Santa Fe today." I said it aloud into the rearview mirror. The scene of sitting on my friend's red porch bench in New Orleans came to mind.

"So, if you can't afford to do Earthship anymore, what are you going to do in New Mexico?" she asked, smacking a mosquito dead against her thigh.

"I am going to get myself to Santa Fe, because it seems really beautiful, stop and turn around, and see what's going on for me, and take it from there," I replied confidently. She nodded her head with a smile and we sat in the sweaty August evening.

I put on my metal yellow aviators, repeated my mantra, "I am going to Santa Fe," and got on the interstate. I pumped myself up with some dub-step songs and the GPS counted down the miles. The sky was a rich blue, filled with possibilities. I was headed to my Airbnb spot, happy and relieved to be back on course. There I would gleefully prepare for my Utah backcountry tryout, shop for the water bladder I needed at REI, and fancifully walk the historic downtown at dusk. Great, I had my plan, back on track, and I'm all good.

I had fifteen miles left. Chevy and I descended a slightly steep grade on the interstate—nothing to be too turned on by. Panic struck, a lightning bolt ignited my heart into hot chaos. No storm tracker warning, no severer weather alert, it just ripped me apart like an F5 tornado. My heart beat at a manic pace. My hands and feet tingled hard and then went totally numb. Numb. The sensation of the gas pedal beneath my right foot vanished.

What the fuck. What the fuck. What-the-fuck-is-going-on?

My cloudy brain couldn't think of anything else to register. It was frozen in fear. I grabbed for my cell phone in the black rubber cup holder. It had service. The tremors of last night returned and I could barely hold onto it. I didn't know whether to keep driving or stop. Chaos raged internally, it was like a rave inside of my body that I hadn't agreed to host. Externally the radio continued to play its dub step and cars still whizzed up the desert interstate.

When you glimpse your own death, when fear paralyzes you, life becomes more urgent.

More…alive.

"Santa Fe 911, what is your emergency," a woman's voice said succinctly. My medical wilderness training kicked in again. I recited the symptoms I was experiencing as clearly as I could in my panicked haze. Invisible scariness all around me.

"I am a twenty-eight-year-old female driving on I-25, my extremities suddenly have gone numb, heart rate super high and I can't catch my breath, tell me what to do!" I pleaded into the phone.

I felt like I was on the phone with God. *"God, is this it? Tell me what to do? I'm afraid to die!"* I was going to die in my car at that moment.

I am dying on my road trip. Right. Now.

I waited for the woman's response and everything moved very slowly. The vanished gas pedal was still under my foot, the cars were still on the road, but it all got very trippy. My mind began to index critical information like a coin sorter. Images of New Orleans went to the dimes, the smell of Thanksgiving at my mom's to the nickels, sounds of Argentinian Spanish trickled into the penny slot. The word fear clogged the system. It appeared in my mind's eye with spectacular clarity. The indexing ceased and a monologue of fear description paraded through my gray matter…

What is the fear? Primal fear. Fear parades around with human body symptoms but churns with spiritual gale force winds. It is so scary. You watch as your skin melts off your flesh. Chakras are being wiped clean. The serpent woman crawls up your spine, reaching like a sexy motherfucker for Source—the only problem is she is trying to do this *within* your physical body. Fear is indicative of real, true, gritty ass growth. You are ascending into a new level of existence. No, sorry, you can't choose when. This isn't an elevator. This is you, lovely spirit being, wearing a human body suit, incarnate in this heavy third dimension. This Ascension business is not the elevator of the Trump tower. You can't just hit 201 and pick the level. All levels are illuminated; you are about to visit every piece of your soul.

Floor. By. Floor.

Fear demands your heart to palpate in murmurs you do not understand and have a sense of death standing behind your body. Fear is ego, and it is not going to die without a knife fight. You are not going crazy. You are surrounded by crazies, riding the Trump elevator, unaware that to be aware is the first floor on the way to reclaiming sanity. Reach deep inside dear one. Grab your guts. Yank on them. Bloodied and gross, grasp your innards and hold on. You are chosen. And you are about to explode. You didn't need the human space suit anymore anyway.

"Ma'am, I need you to pull over right now and get in a position of comfort until my dispatched ambulance comes out," The woman at the other end of the phone spoke with authority, jarring me from my trippy haze.

I obeyed, and happened to be coming up on exit 264. I let the car roll up on the shoulder, put her in park and immediately got out. I didn't want to be in the Chevy another nanosecond.

Getting out of the car on exit 264, a few things happened. The tingling in my extremities subsided and so did my racing heart. The panic haze began to lift. I wrapped my hands behind my head and looked into the desert behind the Chevy. A metaphoric mirage manifested. A familiar crowd of people stood behind the Chevy bent over, panting. I stared at them. Like familiar suitcases on an airport carousel, they were all there; the men of NORP who bullied me every day, Steph, Marcus, my hostile landlord from the overpriced rental, even the divorced marine who wooed me for a nine-month lustful affair. They were all there, staring back at the frail, half-dead former version of me, in the New Mexican desert.

"Finally, you stopped, we were so tired of chasing you and your car," Steph said, speaking for the whole mirage crowd. A cumulative exhale pushed the dry air through the blue desert sky and rattled the wind across the nearby scrub brush.

"I can stop; I want to stop. I want to deal with this," I replied to the crowd. It echoed from my deepest self. The spectacular woman inside the human space suit that was still tripping hard on metaphoric peyote. The truest version of Traci. She was so fucking tired of running after a played out, outdated version of her soul. Something inside clicked. Where the car stopped today, where my body stopped, there was no more sprinting an invisible marathon.

We all must face our own souls and our crowd of wrongdoers. When you do, it will feel like you are dying. Because you are. The old is burning off, baby skin will soon show, and it will need to be cared for gently.

It is said, "When the student is ready, the teacher appears." Sometimes a class reunion is in order.

The sirens of the ambulance pierced the mirage and my crowd of wrongdoers evaporated into the dry air. I stood against the Chevy's trunk, a disheveled wreck. Rattled to my core, sweaty, and tired. An ambulance came up at the front of the car and two state troopers came to the back.

I sputtered the summary of what had happened, and the EMTs gently led me to the back of the ambulance. The inside of the ambulance looked just like the primetime hospital shows—the stretcher right there, sterile cabinets of gauze, needles, and first responder things. The two men asked me to lie on the stretcher and I did. I just wanted to lie down. The blood pressure cuff tightened and loosened around my right arm and my left index finger stung from the bloody fingerpick.

"Miss Traci, do you know the date and where you are?" Bobby the

EMT said. His brown eyes warm and caring.

"It is October first-ish, midday, and I am on my way to Santa Fe," I usually don't know the date, or the day of the week, especially when I'm unemployed, but I did because it was the day of my mother's retirement party.

"Great."

He went on to describe what my experience might have felt like. His story was exactly mine. The tight chest, the feeling of imminent death, the tingling. He mentioned everything except the epic encounter with my mirage of haters. He must live in a McMansion with a place to hold his emotional shit.

"Yes! That is totally how it felt," I said, happy to be affirmed, and skittish for a pending diagnosis. It was as if he watched the whole event unfold across the interstate with binoculars moments before.

"It seems to me you had a panic attack; nothing to be ashamed of," he cautioned, "This happens to huge amounts of people and can occur very randomly. Have you had any recently trauma?" His words clattered around my brain, just like they had the night before.

Recent trauma. Recent trauma. The slideshow in my mind's eye began. *The day Reggie asked me which sex position I preferred. The days spent eating lunch alone so I didn't need to talk to my co-workers. The night Marcus's text message confessional blew up my phone. The brutal four-hour day in Baton Rouge with the HR ladies. Stephanie's empty eyes at my resignation letter. My storage unit.* It all played on loop like bad Christmas music.

The side door of the ambulance whipped open and a burst of cold air rushed in. A petite but tough state trooper lady walked in and I watched my heart rate spike on the monitor. I had already told the other officer I had taken one of my anti-anxiety medications before I drove, to stave off potential panic.

"Miss Traci, from what you have told Officer Roberta, I am this close to charging you with a DUI," she squeezed her thumb and index finger together in front of her eye. "You could have been driving while impaired, and I cannot let you drive your car any further," she said. She placed her hands on her duty rig and I knew I was in a pickle.

The EMTs and police pow-wowed, leaving me in the ambulance.

Yes, that was dumb. I take medication for Tourette's. I have since I was 14. One time in Guatemala when I had food poisoning and was shitting and vomiting everywhere my pharmacist friend popped me one of my anti-anxiety meds to "bring me back down". It worked then, so I thought it would work now in the desert. The only difference was I was also trying to operate "heavy machinery". It was the pink label "no- no" on the bottle. Oops.

The EMTs worked some magic, just like they do on the ABC primetime dramas, and fended off a felony.

With that, the officer ordered me to arrange Triple A to tow the car into town and I would take an expensive taxi ride with lights and sirens. I ordered the tow, confirmed it with tiny but mighty Officer Roberta and they clipped me into the stretcher for the ride. My tired body sunk into the ever stronger reality of things unfolding. The ride was short. I was checked into the hospital by Bobby and then never saw him again. One hour later an RN about my age, very attractive, wearing a Colorado shirt and a clearance card approached.

"Sweetie, are you the interstate arrival?" she asked.

"Um, yes." I was flattered I had already made a name for myself in Santa Fe, even if it was "the interstate arrival".

"You are all cleared unless you want to check in and be evaluated by a doctor," she offered.

"No thank you, I was already seen last night in Albuquerque," I held out my arm to show her the wristband. I didn't want to be poked or prodded anymore. I needed to rest.

"Okay, well you be careful out there," she rubbed my back and ushered me to the front waiting room.

TRACI ANN

Kindness Is Always Possible
09.30.2014

A gray Crown Vic rolled up to the Santa Fe Medical center with rims that are the old lady kind, the ones that look like bicycle spokes. You know what I am talking about.

Karen had graciously kept herself updated on my whereabouts since I staggered into Albuquerque, so when I called her from the ambulance ride, she was on it.

"Just text me and I will come get you my dear," she said patiently.

I texted her immediately when they cleared me at the hospital and waited out in the high desert dry sunshine for her to come pick me up. There were no clouds. October's beginning made itself known in the cold air flushing my cheeks off the mountains. She got out of the gray Crown Vic and helped me with my backpacks into the car.

"Welcome to Santa Fe, Traci. I am sorry you have had such a hard few days," she pouted her lips into a sad face then quickly morphed her expression into an upbeat smile.

I laughed. "Thank you Karen."

It felt hard to breathe fully, so we talked very gingerly. It was so strange to try and monitor my breath…wondering if I truly had enough of it. I was dazed and traumatized, so ready to rest in the bed she had waiting for me.

"Where is your car?" she asked.

Shit. I forgot about that part. The terrible day that would not end.

"It is at B&G Towing, I called AAA," I said meekly.

"Oh, well we should go get it first, then go home, it is very close," she switched lanes to route us to the towing joint.

We walked into B&G Towing and a guy with a well-manicured chinstrap goatee named Dave was at the desk. The whole office was adorned with 1970s wood paneling and smelled like my grandparents.

"How can I help you, little lady?" Dave said leaning both elbows on the counter at me.

"I called AAA to get my car towed off the interstate earlier and they said it would arrive here, B&G Towing."

His face looked sad as he scrolled the computer screen, trolling for my car information. I had a sinking feeling when we walked in and I didn't see my beloved car-home parked in the yard.

"Sweetie this is B&G Automotive, B&G Towing is across town, let me call them real quick and make sure the car is there," Dave said calmly.

Karen smiled and rubbed my forearm kindly.

"Okay, I'll let her know," Dave hung up the phone in frustration. He had to tell me the bad news. "Traci, your tow got cancelled because the officer, Officer Roberta, she had to go to another call and nobody could stay with the vehicle…and you have the keys." Dave gestured to the carabiner on my jeans.

Fuck. My. Life.

I burst into tears; I sobbed into my dirty, sweaty cotton shirt. What will I do now? I am in no condition to drive, I am not going back down that interstate, that was the scene of the crime. I wailed. It must have sounded like a cat was dying inside the wood paneled office. It came up through my body from the bottom of my feet.

"Sweetheart, we are gonna get your car, don't you worry about a thing." Dave grabbed my other forearm and rubbed it too.

Strangers are friends just waiting to happen.

Mike came in as I was mid sob. He had the same chinstrap goatee Dave did, but he was younger, clearly Hispanic, and hot. I was a hot mess. I was mortified. I used to be an amazing outdoor cool writer chick! I wanted to slip him a note so he knew this wailing broken woman was not my true fierce identity.

"Mike here will ride with Karen and go drive your car back to you," Dave slapped Mike on the back.

I might be a little unsure of which gender I prefer a romp with, but I do know I love when men help out ladies in distress. I was clearly in distress and these strangers were going to travel fifteen miles down the interstate, for free, to go get my car-home. With Karen, another person

I had just met who seemed to be willing to do almost anything to improve my quality of life here in Santa Fe.

Maybe it is the Land of Enchantment.

Karen and Mike dropped me off at a Starbucks near the interstate on-ramp and I bought an expensive organic fruit juice squeezable snack. I slurped it up ravenously, with shaky hands. A few onlookers noticed my hospital bracelet and I could tell they were a bit wary of me. I wondered what they were whispering to each other. For all they knew, I was an escaped hospital crazy lady, spending someone else's money on high-priced baby food labeled as, "organic on-the-go superfood".

I slumped in a comfy chair and tried to feel super. I didn't. I felt super lame. I wanted to shake my head vigorously and be back in New Orleans in my old life. Before the summer. Living with my boss-roommate, cooking dinner, drinking wine, dancing to zydeco at Jazzfest, and co-dependently pretending life was functioning full and well. But it wasn't. Her Peace Corps lover-turned-fiancée was living thousands of miles away in Boston and she was living in New Orleans, anxiously awaiting the June wedding.

After June, they would be a happy married lesbian couple, who would move the whole operation to NOLA and live happily ever after. I would move out and magically find a place to live in NOLA and continue working for her under the guise that bullying at work and sexual language was okay. Together we inadvertently wove a very complex web between our separate lives. The neighbors thought I was her future wife due to the engagement announcement and the timing of when I moved in.

"Well you must be the lucky lady!" one of Stephanie's neighbors announced at me as I was walking her dog up the street after work one day last April. Peanut sniffed the new flowers eagerly, uninterested by the conversation.

"Excuse me?" I said, whistling for Peanut to come back a bit before we continued the walk.

"The wedding! Stephanie definitely found a looker, about time." The short lady clamored with her mail back into her house before I could explain I was indeed not the fiancée but the poor employee Stephanie had agreed to house.

The idea that any of our lives are separate is horseshit. Nobody on this planet is separate; we are all connected, and involved. It's just we, Stephanie and I, probably could have set better boundaries—such as *everything*. But hindsight is 20/20 and magic is always there, you just need to stay present and aware.

You also should never live with your boss. Or sleep with them. Just don't do it. I never did the latter, but living with her changed my life enough.

I heard a horn beep outside of Starbucks and it sounded familiar. My car! I walked outside and hot Mike was in the Chevy's driver seat. Magic floated around me. I was present.

Mike waved from his buddy's car as they drove away from Karen's home. The yellow quaking Aspen leaves flickered the sunset on the adobe home. I stood in the early evening air in a state of grace and bewilderment.

I just got my car off the interstate for free, evaded a DUI for popping an anti-anxiety med before I drove, got a safe ride into Santa Fe, and an equally amazing treatment from Marc in Albuquerque less than twenty-four hours before.

Why do strangers perform magic tricks for others? I had been the recipient of so much random kindness, no wonder my mind was mush. I went to walk inside of Karen's house to collapse in the guestroom when my phone buzzed. It was Marc.

Marc: *Traci, its Marc from ABQ, from the hospital last night, I want to make sure you are okay and made it to Santa Fe, please let me know if you need anything.*

What else is possible when you are down to nothing? Kindness is always possible, that's for sure.

Netflix Sex
10.1.14

Karen is an old lady with white long braided hair and three cats. Karen talks to herself, and laughs out loud while quilting in her extra room, but that's okay because she saved my life for the mere price of $40 per night, which includes lemon poppy-seed muffins and breakfast frittata if I ever decide to eat again. Yesterday, after all the panic, after all the mysterious miracles of people helping me, it felt like an old part of my brain died. Like an outdated version of the Oregon Trail that didn't work on the new PCs that came out in the '90s, my circuitry doesn't connect anymore. I lay here in Santa Fe, so dumbfounded. Something doesn't work anymore; I can't ford the river on this one...I need to jump into the current, my oxen peaced-out yesterday.

I am filled to the brim with fear. Not because I am in a strange home in Santa Fe with a generous woman who is mildly under constant, self-imposed cabin fever, but because of the panic.

I lay in the cozy bed, immobilized by fright, and also by sheer exhaustion. A captive to my own terror, I pondered my prison. It is actually quite posh. The room has barren taupe-colored walls, super soft bed sheets, a black leather recliner, and a sweet Keurig machine with tea K-cups next to it on a display tree.

I rolled on my side, pulled the covers over my ears, and thought of Joseph Campbell; the famous mythologist whose idea of the "hero's journey" is quasi-mainstream now. The hero's journey is a process that each human being has a chance to engage in and it is the highest honor. It is said that the climax of the hero's journey is the battle; one battles the fear of death. And once that battle is fought within the veiled realm of one's mind, that the hero transmutes the fear into joy and then into unrelenting life enthusiasm. The hero then no longer fears death and he or she is fearless.

Without fear. Sans scaredy cat. *Nada meidoso.*

When fear throws down, we must prepare the arms, our truth is to be fearless…it is a destiny hoped for by the Universe for every human being.

Based on the puffiness under my eyes and body aches, I believe I waged a battle yesterday on the highway. I feared death yesterday. I wanted to stay alive so much, I fought fear like a motherfucker.

Last night I wanted to sleep off the panic like a bad college night of drinking. One of those idiotic nights when you mix liquors, beer, and shit out of a garbage can from the frat boys' house. Sleep doesn't come when you panic, or mix liquor and beer when you are in college. Fear waits for you like an ominous dark spirit you foolishly can only describe as something reminiscent of the Hamburglar, since you are a newbie to this whole fight or flight thing when there is no actual bear to run away from.

I lay in my Airbnb bed, the thin New Mexico air vented through the blinds, giving the room a fresh morning glow. I felt pathetic though; a failure, a pile of stinky poo. Only my father knew what had happened. My mother was in the middle of her surprise retirement party, when I was in the middle of my surprise hero's journey battle on I-25. I entrusted my dad to tell her what had occurred yesterday. I was ashamed on a certain level and also a smidge happy. Strangely relieved. Something ended yesterday. I could stop running. I could choose to face my demons and work through my baggage.

We always have a choice. Today I chose Netflix.

For my first day of recovery I decided to engage in my first ever TV series marathon. I am not much of a TV watcher, but I needed something mindless, yet stimulating and entertaining. I clicked on *Orange is the New Black* and indulged in woman-on-woman goings-on. Something to focus on that wasn't my train wreck life. Hot women, kissing and fucking in a prison, under hilarious terms, proved to be just the recovery remedy. Episode after episode I drifted further into the plot, and further into my own sexuality. I danced around it flirtatiously; letting myself enjoy watching ladies kiss each other, liberated from self-judgment for a fleeting moment.

I contemplated the first time I would go on a date with a lady and not text my boyfriend to rescue me. The first time I would kiss a woman. I am a great kisser. She will be stunned, whoever she is.

Maybe I won't like it; maybe this is all just a farce I have created because I am tired of tactless men and the way a man looks naked with a flaccid penis. It is so gross. A naked man, without an erect penis, from the waist down is kind of anti-climactic. The body of a woman is so enchanting, so curvy, whimsical and unexpected, so sacred. It could be I am making up the denial too. Either way, this is not a battle I want to have a scissor fight with today. So I just watch another episode and drink tea in my cocoon-room filled with homemade quilts.

I wanted to masturbate when I watched one of the main characters receive some killer oral sex but my heart rate was already abnormally high just sitting in the black recliner. It still hadn't regulated itself since yesterday's affairs. That was the first time I was able to empathize with the man's voice on the Viagra commercial when he says, "Please consult your doctor to make sure your heart is healthy enough for sex." At the moment my heart is not healthy enough for sex. Not even sex with my Netflix.

Alas, horny and frustrated I stayed, drifting in and out of half-sleep naps. When Karen knocked on the door the room was dimly illuminated in natural light.

"How you doing? Boy, you slept all day!" Karen held onto the door, peeking in at me from the hallway.

"Yeah, I still feel tired," I said, letting a yawn escape.

"Would you like some chicken soup? I just made it," Karen's voice was coaxing; she knew I hadn't eaten all day. "C'mon out of here and fix yourself a bowl," she continued, pushing the door open and letting the delightful soup smell pour into my room.

"Okay, that sounds great actually," I replied. I put on my sweatshirt and went into the kitchen for the soup. All three cats eyed me from various posts in the kitchen as I ladled myself a microscopic portion of soup. I slurped it slowly and Karen watched with approval from her quilting chair in the living room.

"That a girl," she said.

I returned to my cocoon room for the rest of the evening, enjoying one more show before bedtime. Nightfall came and I prayed for actual sleep. The future, beyond whether or not Piper would get back with Alex, my future, felt like a free fall down a well.

There is Still Work to be Done
10.2.14

The heat roused me. I think my cell phone said 4:15 a.m. My heart pounded and I realized I was having some sort of anxiety aftershock. That last episode of *Orange is the New Black* was just too much before bed I suppose.

Regardless I am panicked. I remembered suddenly about belly breathing; a way to breathe solely from your stomach as not to agitate your already tight chest. A way to inhale deeper, to get more oxygen. This wasn't a full blown one I could tell; it was a feeling of agitation and a passing hot flash of sorts that stirred me out of a full sleep.

I walked carefully into the bathroom and ushered out one of Karen's black cats with my foot. It meowed loudly before scooting up the dark hallway. I shut the door and laid on the cool tile.

"Breathe Traci, let it come and let it go," a voice inside my head said.

So I did. The discomfort was gross, my throat muscles automatically prepared to release vomit, so I leaned over the toilet. Nothing happened. No puke. I laid back down on my back and concentrated on filling my stomach up with air slowly; I watched it rise and fall under my small hands. I did my best to ride the wave.

I slipped in and out of what looked to be film shorts of my previous life chapter. Inhale and Marcus's onslaught of text messages came together in my mind's eye. Ten of them. All one after the next, like soldiers marching through my phone. I was still living at my boss-roommate's place when it happened. Still being bullied by day, and in the evening excitedly planning for my summer trip to Costa Rica for my other education gig. Costa Rica would turn this around, it would give me the space I needed to decide whether or not to continue working for a boss who didn't hear the cries for help against a backdrop of disrespectful men.

Why do we do this as women? We must create time and space to *think* about whether or not to leave a clearly shitty life scenario. My husband hit me a few times. I feel if I go on this weekend yoga retreat it will give me the clarity I need to *think* about potentially leaving him. My boyfriend cheated on me, but it was the first time. I will go visit my sister in New York and *think* about what I should do. We are all horribly stuck in outlandish holding patterns of fucked-up societal beliefs about where we should be, especially as women. The only place we need be is where we can give and receive loving kindness from our fellow humans. Let the abusers and jackasses go meditate somewhere and get clarity. You already have the answer you seek, fellow wayfarer; it is encoded in your DNA, you need not search for it at your sister's in New York. It is called self-respect and we all must give it to ourselves, especially when we doubt we should be the recipients.

I looked up at the bathroom ceiling and watched Marcus's text messages appear.

Marcus: *Hi Traci, sorry to bother you in the middle of your evening but I need to get something off my chest.*

Marcus: *I have feelings for you, romantic feelings, and they will not go away.*

Marcus: *I needed to share this with you, lest it stay buried inside of me forever. You represent the ideal woman I am searching for. You are extremely gorgeous, funny, ambitious, and intelligent. You know what you want and you go for it.*

Marcus: *I don't know what will come of me telling you this, but I needed to, and get it off my chest. I just didn't want to express my feelings in a deeper way physically in person. I know nothing can come of it as I am a married man with children.*

Marcus: *I love you Traci, I really do, I don't know what to do. Please don't tell Stephanie.*

I read those text messages over and over again in Stephanie's kitchen. Each time a different emotion emerged. First surprise. Then disbelief. Fear floated. Anger loomed. Ego-driven self-indulgence came for me like the devil, and then gravity drove me into the ground like a pile. I stood over Stephanie's granite countertop, hunched over, tears in my eyes. I could hear her in her bedroom, on Skype, talking to her future wife.

So close we were, I thought. My boss and I, my friend. I stood in her kitchen, a place we normally kept warm with conversation about the city and life, yet that night the kitchen was icy and isolated.

"Please don't tell Stephanie," fluttered. It stung. I wanted to tackle Stephanie, slam her throat against the headboard of her bed and hold my cell phone up to her face. Make her hang up the Skype phone with her fiancée and say, "Read this! Your prized worker, your golden work boy, is making my life a living hell!" I wanted her to acknowledge the mess I was in. To seek counsel, to be consoled. Yet I did not. I wrote some bullshit back to Marcus to hold off his text messages and went outside and fell apart.

I walked up to the bayou two blocks away, laid in the grass and cried my face off. Then I walked back, got in my car, switched on the headlights, and turned the music up real loud. I screeched up the interstate, all the windows down, trying to wash the filth of my ill-informed co-worker off me. I sped past the Superdome, all lit up with fun colors of spring, and realized fully that the universe was asking me to do the hardest thing to date. To recognize the death of my life in New Orleans. To leave. It was time to be open for something more.

Something better than a great job, but shitty co-workers. Something better than living cheaply with my boss from her kindness, but leading a double life. Something better than attracting a married man with two wonderful kids to me. It was time to leave New Orleans for good.

I didn't need to decide what to do, the decision was already in my soul, I just needed to stoke the courage fire long enough to start an inferno large enough that it caught my attention.

The tile felt so good against my hot angry slideshow of the previous months. I let the text message blunder fall from the ceiling and melt onto the ceramic. I tried to forgive, but noticed my body wasn't there yet. I tried to forgive my boss-roommate too, but that was another absolution that hadn't cooked fully in my being yet.

At first frustration laid on top of anger. "Why can't I forgive them yet? I want to heal—that is why I am on this trip traveling west, to *healllll*!" My self-talk was noticeably intense. I swore Karen would wake up at any moment.

We are our biggest critics.

A gentler, truer woman stepped into the internal dialogue. She didn't really speak at first. She climbed out of my belly button and was carrying a big stick. She walked up to me, panting on the ceramic tile floor that smelled like kitty litter, and leaned my head down, putting my ear closer to the ground. I thought I might get scolded with her stick. On the contrary. This mini woman, very reminiscent of myself, carrying a stick, said, plainly, "Because there is more work to do. You forgive effortlessly when the inner work gets done."

And then, she walked away. She climbed up my sweatpants and jumped back down my belly button.

It was probably approaching 5:30 a.m. when I finally sat up off the cool tile floor. I looked around the bathroom. I was still in New Mexico at Karen's. My heart rate was slower and I still had not forgiven myself, Marcus, Stephanie, or the other snotballs I worked with.

Clearly I still had a lot of work to do. I crawled back into bed and found my way into a deep, finally restful, sleep.

Wishbone and Santa Fe Spirits

10.3.14

Calmer today. I ate a fried egg for breakfast and used the remaining instant Nescafe-mixed-with-hazelnut-coffee-creamer that was in my grocery bag. Camping in Big Bend, dancing under the Marfa sky, feeling free and not captive to my mind...these things were light-years away.

Am I crazy? Will I always be crazy now? Will I make it home to New York safely?

After hours of deliberations and permutations of a game plan, my dad and I had decided on a positive next step: I would fly home to Albany from Albuquerque, and dad would arrange a car hauler to come bring the Chevy to Florida. My parents are about to join the ranks of snowbird New Yorkers who migrate bi-annually to Florida when the skies turn forever gray in upstate New York. I am to road-trip down with them before Christmas to go and retrieve my car. Yeah I know, the last thing I want or need is another road trip at the moment. Minute by minute. I'm confident we'll cover that once I get home.

Since breakfast went over well, I was energized. I decided to leave my Airbnb kingdom-prison and travel to Whole Foods. The car felt normal to get into, though a small amount of unknown Hamburglaresque fright haunted me. Three miles later I parked the Chevy in the overflow lot and ventured inside. The goal of the day was simple: leave the fortress, go get food more substantial than instant camp coffee, and go from there.

When life levels you, you begin again by laying the foundation. Smaller goals, smaller progress. Fashion a simple ladder with what you have, deep in the hole you are in, and slowly you will be able to climb out. At least that is what I am hoping.

I traipsed around the sparkly, fall decorated Whole Foods in a quasi-zombie state, grateful to be alive and breathing but scared to be

193

around people, embarrassed I might freak out. My eyes took in all the products with a whirlwind of gratitude flushing my system. The eggs, the Kombachu, the perfectly colorful produce, the free samples. My senses were overloaded; everything was vibrant and overwhelming in a way I had never experienced before.

"Can I please have the turkey brie Panini?" I ordered from the lady at the sandwich counter.

"Sure, Dijon mustard okay?" she asked, deftly slicing the Panini bread in front of me.

"Yes ma'am," I said, stretching to be heard over the glass counter on my tip toes.

"You just taking your lunch break sweetie? You look tired," The Whole foods lady said, looking at me with true empathy, squirting the Dijon on my sandwich.

"Ah, yeah, kinda," I responded dully, not wanting to fully engage. With any human being. Not yet. Too soon. The sight of the ambulance flashed across my forehead and I swore she could see it. She knows.

"Here you go, sweetheart." She presented the turkey sandwich to me in a foil wrap.

"Thank you," I mustered the best fake smile I could.

"Now go get some rest!" She remarked, shooing me away with a motion of the hand.

I took my sandwich, grabbed a $6 bottle of organic, allegedly magical apple cider, with added glitter or something hokey, and gingerly wandered to the register. I got my change and posted up inside, setting up my sandwich and fancy apple cider on the lunch bar that overlooked the main entrance.

Bite by bite. Minute by minute. Surrender is so powerful. So was the power I felt sitting in Whole Foods nourishing my body after a mess of seventy-two hours. I tried to wrap my head around how in under five days I secured and then lost a promising job tryout in Utah four days from now. With the new game plan, Utah was obviously out of the question. I emailed Ben last night regretfully informing him I could no longer attend the tryout due to a "family emergency". It sucked so hard to write that email, but I know deeply the universe is rife with miracles and somehow, it would all work out. Canceling the tryout now, pre-emptively, was better than being in the backcountry and having the panic Hamburglar come to visit me in my tent halfway to Zion National Park.

I let my brain reel a little, heart rate still in an elevated thump. I looked out the window and watched the cars go up and down Cerrillos road. I took a swig of my luscious, cold pressed cider and noticed a small white dog dancing in the traffic. *Shit, now I really am hallucinating.* Must be the $6 apple cider with organic glitter.

But I wasn't hallucinating. There was indeed a dog running across the busy main road of Santa Fe! He looked like the dog from a childhood TV show I grew up on, Wishbone. Wishbone was a precious little Jack Russell terrier who talked and educated youths like me about literary classics by dressing up in doggie Don Quixote outfits. It held my attention so much so that I watched it every day after school and found the intellectual Jack Russell very captivating.

This dog was Wishbone, after the show got cancelled on PBS; homeless or a runaway in need of a bath and some TLC. He darted left and right, finally making it to the parking lot entrance of Whole Foods. He wore a silver choke chain and a faded white rope that looked like it had been yanked free.

Why does a weary traveling woman, fresh from the hospital, decide to race outside—er, speed walk—to save a mangy dog who looks like Wishbone? Besides an autograph? Because it is human instinct to help. We all want love, and we all want to serve. That's why we are here.

"Could you watch my purse and stuff for a second?" I asked quickly to the woman sitting next to me at the lunch counter. "There is a loose dog running around in the traffic outside," I continued, already halfway out the door.

"Sure, I'll be here," she replied.

I walked over to the dog as fast as my racing heart would allow and whistled at him. He turned, in the middle of peeing on a low shrub, and wagged his tail hard. He came right over and licked my face. I grab his rope while we were making out—guys are so easily distracted—and suddenly I had a new piece of life: a rescued look-a-like of Wishbone who needed a bath, some water, and a way home.

When you have no idea what to do, just keep walking.

I walked Wishbone back over to the Whole Foods outdoor patio and was immediately rushed with compliments about "my dog" from strangers.

"What a sweet pea!" said a mom with a child in a stroller.

"Aww what a good looking dog, so cute, how old is he?" A man asked who had just rolled up on a bicycle.

"I have no idea...he isn't mine," I replied blankly. Wishbone looked back and forth at us, wagging his tail all over the place.

"Huh?" The man took off his helmet slowly.

"I am not from around here; I just came to town. I was eating lunch inside and saw him cross four lanes of traffic," I said, hoping he might help.

Wishbone peed on the man's shoes and back bike tire. I turned away trying to stifle my smile and laughter.

"I'm sorry about that. My name is Traci," I said, offering my free hand that wasn't all dirty from Wishbone's grimy body.

"Aaron," he said warmly with a smile and gray hair swaying in the warm air. Aaron looked about to be in his late thirties.

Everyone was so helpful in Santa Fe. Since the day I rolled into town, panic aside, all my social interactions have been downright pleasant. They all have a spiritual buzz humming around them. Maybe the apple cider really is magical. The lady who was watching my purse and lunch brought everything outside where Wishbone, Aaron, and I sat, searching for animal controls number on our phones.

"Looks like you found a new friend," she knelt down beside us and stroked the top of my new dog's head. Wishbone licked her ankle. "I bet he's thirsty, I'll be right back," she said, slipping back into the store. She returned with a bottle of water and a bowl. Wishbone chugged the water like a champ, or like a dog who had jumped out of his owner's car three days ago.

"I have an idea!" Aaron said optimistically, when we couldn't find a working number for any area animal rescue. "There is a pet store two blocks up, let's bring him there, they'll know what to do." Such cheerful, hopeful folks, these new people from the Land of Enchantment.

Wishbone must have been feeling content, because he wouldn't budge from his water bowl on the sunny Whole Foods patio. I scooped him up, hoping not to suddenly get bit; that's all I would have needed, another hospital drive-through for rabies. Thankfully he sunk into my arms, trembling, and we walked to the store. Aaron walked his bike over with us.

"So you like to bike I assume?"

"Yes! I love to bike. Actually I just got back from a cycling trip in Canada," Aaron said, slapping the seat of his bike in affection. "Did some great routes through Toronto."

We opened the door to the pet store and a small golden bell acknowledged our entrance. I placed Wishbone on the ground and he began sniffing the air eagerly.

"Well what do we have here?" An older woman in sweater inquired from the back counter. She got down on her knees, I let go of the little rope, and Wishbone ran at her. He jumped onto her lap and licked her face with glee.

"I found him near Whole Foods, he was dodging traffic on Cerrillos," I said.

"No! It's a miracle he made it across without being hit!" Another younger girl chimed in from a nearby shelf of dog food she was stocking. She turned to hear more of the story.

"Can you help us? I am traveling through town and don't know what to do?" I asked.

"Yes of course, a handsome dog like this can't stay on the street," the older lady answered me while still receiving kisses from the charming Wishbone.

Service was expedient at the pet store. These ladies knew how to get things done. Aaron and I stood back as the younger woman looked through a binder briefly and then got on her cell phone. The older woman fed Wishbone sticks of Pupperoni.

"Yes, yes, I will have them go there," the younger girl hung up the phone. "They said to bring him back to Whole Foods and they will come out to get him in about twenty minutes."

"Great, thank you so much," Aaron said, holding the door open for me.

"For the road," the older woman said with a wink. She handed me two additional chewy rawhide treats.

Aaron went inside and bought two ginger beers and setup two chairs in the late afternoon shade, and we tied Wishbone to the heavy chair. A part of me didn't want to give him up. I felt a bond to him; we were both scared and alone in a world of churning uncertainty…maybe we could help each other. I knew it wasn't possible, but his fleeting kisses and cuddles softened the blow of our cumulative uncertainty.

"You know Santa Fe was founded by St. Francis of Assisi, the patron saint of animals. That's why this town is such an animal loving place. Anybody you would have met today would have helped," Aaron took a swig of his ginger beer and smiled cheerfully at me.

Twenty minutes later a lady in a cop-like uniform put a waxy white and blue rope around Wishbone and away he went. I gave him a kiss on the head and we locked eyes.

"Everything will be just fine," I cooed and held his head in my hands.

"Thank you for doing this, we will find a good home for him," the lady in the cop uniform replied.

Why do we say this when we have no idea if things will be fine, or even what fine denotes? I felt lame. I had rescued him, came in hot like superwoman and now I had to give him to the universe. To relinquish control, that was the order of the day for both Wishbone and I. He pranced away with the tall animal control lady, looking back once, giving me a final wag of his tail in gratitude.

Afterwards Aaron and I sat in the patio for another hour or so. His caring, unassuming nature made me feel safe. Everything started to pour out. *Harassed. New Orleans. All things in storage. The instinctive drive west. Panic attack. Ambulance. Altitude. Blood. Apple cider with glitter.*

Two tears finished off the monologue and I didn't know what would happen next…I just felt so alone.

Sweet soul that he was, he didn't move a muscle. He listened with his whole body, leg crossed towards me, leaning in, the whole bit. When I was done, he handed me a tissue and waited for me to blow my nose.

"Traci. First off, I thought you were from somewhere like California. You are so laid back," he leaned back in his chair with ease, "And second, please don't worry about a thing. I detect a strong energy from you. Things look bleak now, sure, but you are going to be so much more than fine. Life is strange. Life works out. You will come back to Santa Fe when it is time. You are on the path." And with that, he took our empties and tossed them into the glass receptacle like the good, crunchy guy he was. I was at a loss for what to say.

"It has been a pleasure, know you will be okay, and welcome to Santa Fe," Aaron said. He freed his bicycle from its kickstand and rode off.

After sitting with Aaron and his mysteriously uplifting advice, I felt serene. I surrendered further into my chair and knew deeply, even though there might be pain at every corner still, I would truly make it through this random speed bump of life better than ever.

I drove successfully to downtown to spend the waning hours of the late afternoon and dusk. Everything appeared dreamy. Crisp, staggering sunset. The plaza of historic Santa Fe. The clanging bells of the basilica. I glowed for a reason unknown to me. Everything in the Santa Fe plaza reminded me of another piece of my life. The memories jumped off the mental flipbook and danced tango on the bricked street as an accordion player took me back to Buenos Aires. Walking past open air art galleries, I was transported back to the rich galleries I had spent so much time in while studying in Italy. But I was still just standing on the cobblestone streets of Santa Fe.

Have you ever felt like life is merely replaying different parts of itself over and over again? As if time is not linear? It is all happening at the same time. I am never not in Buenos Aires or Santa Fe, or Italy, we are always everywhere…because we are absolute existence.

An old bearded man in a rocking chair invited me to sit down at his gallery's front entrance on San Francisco Street. Together we watched the dark come and the universe painted the sky in watercolors of blues, oranges, and a calming purple. I felt quiet. Finally, a moment of composure. My heart didn't beat as fast and I wanted it to stay that way forever. I rocked in the rocker next to the gallery owner and witnessed absolute existence.

No, Thank You
10.4.14

I have booked my $500 ticket home to New York to seek safe space with my mom and dad. The flight departs Albuquerque on Monday at nine in the morning, less than seventy-two hours from now. My dad arranged a car carrier truck to come and ship my car to Florida tomorrow, for a grand. In one month I have effectively spent all of my travel money and my life is suggestive of a roller coaster that is under construction and they have run out of track. I am coming up on the part where the track runs out and I am the only one sitting in the entire ride. That's because this is my ride, my life.

Since Whole Foods was such a smash hit for me yesterday, and I felt a certain sense of safety and warmth there, I went back today. Having less fear of impending panic attacks, I again drove the three miles to my new favorite spot in Santa Fe. Today I felt stronger, and hungrier than I had been in days.

I ordered a slice of fresh hot pizza from the stone oven and treated myself to a pumpkin spice latte. Pizza and coffee has always been a weird flavor combination I have enjoyed since college. I had been abstaining from caffeine out of fear of a racing heart and ending up on Karen's ceramic tile floor again. Today felt different. Roller coaster or not, I needed to keep living.

I brought my computer to Whole Foods, set up my work/eating station, and didn't look for any dogs to save. I wanted to save myself, so I began to write. I wrote some poetry, and some of what you have been reading inside of this book.

A fellow traveling friend called and I recounted to her the harrowing tale of my last few days of agony, panic, and Netflix. She listened intently and asked me if I thought it would happen again. If I thought another anxiety attack would happen again? At that very

201

moment my pizza became dramatically less appetizing and stunning red agitation scurried through my body. Hot embers were being stoked, disturbed from their slumber. I had not *thought* about having another panic attack.

I told her I needed to go, and prematurely ended the conversation. The volcano that I had so recently become aware of inside my body mere days ago was active and ready to blow again.

Maybe it was the caffeine. Maybe it was the greasy pizza. Maybe you can talk yourself into anxiety. Regardless, it was bloody happening. My desire to write flatlined and my heart did repeated somersaults in my chest. I walked around Whole Foods, feeling helpless, doing some belly breathing. Ladies out for their Saturday afternoon grocery shop looked at me funny when I walked past them with very clear fear in my eyes. Rather than ask if I was alright, they went about their day, bypassing me for the corral of shopping carts. They put festive pumpkins in their carts while I rode the roller coaster to nowhere.

Fifteen minutes went by and it felt like the apocalyptic Marfa storm that had passed by the festival—a weird memory, never actually producing any rain, but now it was gone. I wanted to drive home, to Karen's safe home, and curl myself up into a super tight ball. Fear is a crazy thing. This fear volcano inside of me was puzzling beyond belief.

I was halfway back to Karen's. Actually, the GPS said four minutes, and it showed a little green dot to indicate the road was devoid of any traffic. My internal volcano erupted, four minutes away from Karen's house. It took the form of a rapid heart rate, a recollection of what an increased heart rate and driving can do to one in Santa Fe, and then shortness of breath. I wanted badly to force my way through it. To "arrive at my destination," with the GPS cheerfully congratulating me at a job well done. But I didn't. I made a fast-braking right hand turn into a medical plaza, parked the car, and did a duck and roll landing, on my feet.

Fuck you panic! Fuck you! I yelled at the volcano inside. But sadly I knew that throwing a tantrum was not going to get the trifecta of mind, body, and spirit on a page of unison and love.

Our bodies are incredible, what they can hold onto and what gets activated and reactivated, even at a cellular level when we have not taken the time to sift through our shit. Sure, it sucks balls, but at least our bodies tell us important things.

I recalled what I had researched online so far about panic. One cannot die from a panic attack. That they are temporary moments of high discomfort, not danger.

Everything is temporary.

So there I was, walking around a grouping of red brick medical buildings. There was a Chiropractic office, an aromatherapy spa, a dentist, and a psychologist office. All of which were closed because it was Saturday afternoon. Lap after lap I slowly strolled around the sidewalks that had shade; it was too hot to stand directly in the sun. Every time my anxiety got turned down to a simmer, I crept over to my beloved car, in an attempting to quietly sneak in the four minute ride up the street. Each time I turned the ignition key, anxiety woke up like a cranky newborn, sending me flying back out of the car and onto the sidewalk. I was a robot short-circuiting; somebody had torn off my metal back panel and was fucking with the red and blue wires.

I tried five times within one and a half hours to find the gumption inside of myself to get into the Chevy and drive the four minutes of green-dot route back to Karen's. The downward spiral of thoughts continued until I was finally too tired to care that I had again gotten myself and my car stranded in Santa Fe.

I sat down on a bench and cried. There was nothing much else to do. To just give in and yield to what was. Self-judgment is such a jerk during these times, especially when you must surrender such a delicate portion of yourself. I rested my tired face in my hands and sobbed. I thought I might very well sleep on the bench at the red brick medical center. The idea of this made me laugh for the first time in a while. Finally, a softening, or truly heading towards the loony bin.

"Are you alright?" A man's voice interrupted my peculiar combination of sobs and laughter. A silver haired man was standing at his green sedan, parked just in front of the bench. It was the only other car in the medical plaza besides mine.

"No, I am having an anxiety attack, I just started getting them, and

I don't know what to do…" I said, totally devoid of any human force. I dropped my head, utterly defeated.

"Oh! Do you need me to call you an ambulance?" he asked, whipping out a cell phone.

I laughed at him. He looked super confused. The last thing I wanted was another valet service from my local EMT friends again.

"No, no," I held up my hand in protest, "I was just at the hospital for this the other day. I just need to get back to where I am staying, I can't drive my car right now," I motioned to my car without looking up.

"Oh! Okay, well, tell me where to take you and we can go right now," he smiled and opened the passenger side door to his green sedan.

Tim is the dentist that inhabits the red brick medical plaza and was staying late to do his quarterly financials. He just happened to stay past the lunch hour to finish up his last few spreadsheets.

I thanked him with one of those awkward car hugs where you are still in your seatbelt.

I walked into Karen's house around four o'clock, grateful she was out somewhere, only because I was mortified at my mental state. I didn't want her to know I got my car stuck again, I didn't want to ask for help. It seemed all my helpers had already done their duties in saving my crazy ass in Santa Fe.

How much help are we ever allowed to ask for? I am beginning to understand the answer is: as much as we need.

My phone buzzed. A Facebook message. The magic factor got turned up ten notches. It was Bryce Wilson.

Bryce and I had met two years ago when we were both backpacking around Nicaragua. We share a passion for writing, travel, and attempting to boogie board at high tide and look like fools. We also, from what I could remember between the cheap red wine and pizza, shared some serious sexy times on a beach on the Pacific Rim that year. Bryce is sexy in this brooding way; evocative of Raphael of the Ninja Turtles—rough around the emotional edges, and possessing a cute, spontaneous flair.

The last Bryce and I talked it was in the spring, on an off, exchanging literary works over email for supportive critique. This was *after* I turned down his offer to ride on the back of a motorcycle he was driving around Central America. If I have one regret, it will probably be not fully honing my naive twenty-something self for one more romp of impulsive sexy travels. But alas, I didn't go on that trip with him last winter. I moved into Stephanie's house and languished in my ill-fated job.

Bryce: *Hey Trace, are you in Santa Fe? I keep seeing your photos on Instagram. I am on a road trip in the US as well and currently in Santa Fe. Staying at the Pecos Inn, gonna watch some football tonight at a bar, if you want to join. No cell phone. Room 115, just come by and knock.*

My jaw dropped. In happiness and awe. Bryce! Excitement. Bryce! Hope. Bryce! Magical person who might possibly be kind enough to come help me get the stranded six-cylinder car-house I left at the red brick medical plaza. Synchronicity is amazing.

I slide open my phone to write him a message in reply and blew my nose, clearing away all the crying residue, making room for another miracle.

Traci: *Bryce! Hey there, I really need you right now. I was very close to where I am staying here in Santa Fe and I got all amped up with anxiety and had to pull over. I have had a few anxiety episodes as I have been driving and can't shake 'em. I need to go get my car, but really need someone to drive with me. If you get this, can you come to where I am staying, and we can go get my car? Please say yes and I will owe you a big hug.*

I hit send and said a prayer to the universe. Hoping so much he would swoop in and save my tired self. And swoop he did. My phone buzzed in a muffled way against the pillow.

Bryce: *No problem, give me the address and I'll be there as soon as I can.*

One hour later the car was back parked on Karen's street and I was having a sunset picnic with the writer I had rolled around in Central American sand with two years ago.

"Do you want to go grab a beer somewhere?" Bryce said after we safely got the car back. Karen ended up helping because I was still very rattled.

"Nah, I'd rather not be around a ton of people, but we can sit outside here and talk?" I pulled my green and red fleece blanket out of the Chevy's trunk and laid it on the sidewalk, facing the dry sky that was waiting to catch the sun as she set on the blue horizon. I also grabbed a box of crackers, trying to be a good host.

Sweet and hard as ever to read, Bryce accepted my invitation, and committed to my outdoor picnic of crackers and water.

"Alright, so the last time we really talked was last January when you dropped me on the plan of riding through Nicaragua with me on the bike. Ever since then your messages were brilliant poems filled with man anger and now you are in front of me talking about panic attacks. What happened to you this year?" Bryce delivered his synopsis all in one dramatic breath.

Oh sweetheart, if life would just give *all of us* the Cliffsnotes version.

His prompt unleashed two hours of (mostly me) talking, explaining, crying, and trying to justify why I didn't go on the uber-spontaneous trip with him, and instead chose to lead my double life in New Orleans, only sixty-five percent happy most days.

It is so powerful to bear witness to your own story. The more it is told, the more power it is given...the power it so naturally should receive. As we tell our story we also reclaim personal power. My story is an honorable one, so is Bryce's and so is yours, dear reader. The moment we hide it, stifle it, judge it too lame to share, we begin a long march down a dead end street. You can always turn around, it's just, if you can avoid walking the dead end street of tiresome self-judgment at the beginning, then you don't have to walk as far.

I curled into Bryce's navy blue fleece jacket just a little bit harder as the streetlight flicked on with a yellow glow. I asked him to hold me.

Not because I wanted our track record to upgrade to rolling around the sidewalks of Santa Fe. But because I had a guttural need to be held. To be held by a man, by the moon, by existence. I just wanted life and its inhabitants to hold me for a hot second.

We sat huddled together in the cold breeze on my blanket. My tears got cold. I dissolved into my story a touch further and acceptance trickled through me. Not full on I accept-myself-even-though-I-stayed-in-an-unhealthy-job-for-way-too-long acceptance. It was the first step. A baby step towards growth and personal vibrational evolution.

"I used to get panic attacks when I was in high school because of overbearing teachers, coaching, and my own self-pressure," Bryce offered, breaking our cuddled silence. "It felt like I was running off a cliff."

His description sounded painfully familiar, so I kept listening, hoping for an enchanted cure. A witch doctor in Santa Fe he knew about and we could go see tomorrow.

"What did you do?" I asked.

"Once I realized I wouldn't die from them, I went into it further, I would let it flow through me fully…then they sort of just went away. I don't really get them anymore," he shrugged his shoulders and looked up at the sky. I watched his eyes contemplate what to say next, inhaling the cologne smell of his jacket. "What if going into it means you continue on this trip? To feel them even more and keep going, maybe that's where your growth lies." His statement was challenging and acutely devilish.

"I've already made the choice to go home. I need to be in a safe space to deal with past hurts. I'm in some sort of cosmic growth spurt," I crossed my arms in defense, "Anyways, how do you know the journey stops when I go home? Maybe that's just another part of it?" I countered, in a snarky tone. Appalled he thought he had the right to challenge me in such a vulnerable state.

"Only you know that Traci, only you know the path that is most correct for you," Bryce said. "One question though, an idea…since your car is being shipped to Florida tomorrow, and hypothetically you could cancel your ticket to New York, what if we took our road trip together?"

His blue eyes looked smoky against the streetlight glow. "I mean, it's a total synchronicity we are both here doing the same thing. I could drive. We could stop all over the East and I could bring you wherever you needed to go," Bryce laid out the offer in an optimistic tone shrouded in desperation. Then he cloaked it with a twist of manipulation I'm not sure he was aware of, "Your second chance."

Glowing red hostility brewed within me. All I need is another man telling me about second chances and how I missed an opportunity with them. Perhaps Bryce had two reasons to run into me: to save my ass, and help me stand strong in my decisions. He got sent my way as a test again.

I had no desire to ride into the sunset with Bryce. The last opportunity came at a time when I wanted to run away and not face the demons. Again, the same theme, the demons are back and Bryce is selling a way out, a way to sidestep the inner work. I know I didn't do a great job the first time around, six months ago, but I know I made the correct choice in not going with him on the motorcycle adventure.

I inhaled self-acceptance. I breathed out the words, "No, thank you—I am going home to heal," I looked directly in his beautiful eyes and spoke my honesty.

"Okay," Bryce said, not putting up any sort of fight for his grand plan, "Well...I'm going to go watch the football game at the bar," he hugged me before getting into his car. I stayed outside at the sidewalk picnic and watched the stars come out.

I mulled over what Bryce had mentioned about going further into the panic. How can you be the observer, the honorable witness of passing thoughts and actions, when you feel like you are in cardiac arrest? What is waiting on the other side of the fear and panic?

Last Day in Santa Fe
10.5.14

This time tomorrow I will be on a flight back to New York. It is 11 a.m. and I am doing everything I can to deter myself from over-thinking. Or thinking in general. Petrified out of my mind to have another attack, I watched movies to keep me calm. I watched *Maid in Manhattan*, *Pretty Woman*, and *The Wedding Planner*, all movies that would not increase my heart rate in any way; Jennifer Lopez always keeps me calm in her sappy romantic comedies. And no woman can resist Pretty Woman, even if it's the ninety-ninth time it comes on TV.

I am counting down the moments before I can go home. I am also deeply sad that this is happening. Confusion set in a while back, about three anxiety episodes ago, and now I am left with anguish, gaping holes of uncertainty, and a shattered identity.

My phone chimed. It is the truck driver who is coming to pick up the Chevy today.

"I will be there around two o'clock," he said hastily, hanging up the phone before I could say anything.

Karen knocked on the door, and entered my guestroom movie fortress holding a glass of purple grapes. She smiled and hugged me as I sit propped up in the bed with a pillow, computer on my lap. She extended the grapes saying, "These are from my friends' garden."

"Thank you," I answered, pausing *The Wedding Planner*.

"Traci, just so you know, we all prayed for you at church today. I put in a special request and Father Joe made a prayer announcement on your behalf. Everyone at church hopes you return home safe and recover from this minor life setback," Karen said, stroking my hand, sitting on the edge of the bed in mom position.

I teared up with emotion, trying not to break my even keel, lest the volcano inside erupt again. But I couldn't help it. A whole church of strangers are praying for me in Santa Fe? That is truly remarkable and so loving. I sniffed back a few tears and Karen departed for the grocery store after feeding her cats.

My cell chimed again at 2:05.

"Hey, can you drive the car down the hill to the end of the street? I can't make the turn onto your friend's street," the truck driver said in a heavy Spanish accent.

"Yes," I respond automatically.

I temporarily forgot that driving in New Mexico gives me rabid anxiety. I walked out of the room, keys in hand, volcanic lava starting to spew, headed for the front door, when Bryce burst through the door.

Yes, Bryce! Right on time again. Had he slept in the car outside overnight, waiting to see if I had changed my mind about the sexy road trip offer? I had not. And I was ready to throttle him if that is why he ambushed me in Karen's house.

"Hey, can I use the bathroom?" he stammered, looking upset that I had startled *him*.

"Ah, sure, first door on the right," I replied, now very confused. He came across town to use Karen's bathroom?

Whatever the case, his timing was really useful. I asked him for one final, epic drive around in my Chevy, and he said sure. He wheeled the car down the street and we both spent a half hour watching the guy prep, load, and drive the car away to Florida. It felt like I was sending my child off to boarding school. Secretly happy for some alone time, but also terribly guilty. We shared so much—electrical malfunctions in the Chisos, aggressive tire-pumping with Jake, and countless miles of my mind. I will reunite with the Chevy in Florida, I hope so much I am not afraid of her by then. A weight lifted from my chest as my six-cylinder got towed away.

"So, final offer, do you want to come with me on the road trip of a lifetime?" Bryce said with a smug air that was coming from the beers coursing through his Sunday afternoon football system.

The road trip of a lifetime? I think I just experienced that. Without you, sugar. I want the healing adventure of a lifetime...can you drive me into my own depths?

"Final answer, Bryce, is no. I want to slow down, listen to my deepest self, and start untangling some of my stuff," I stood very straight, and puffed my chest a little.

"Well then, I guess this is most likely the last time I will see you then," Bryce's eyes looked defeated and epically lonely. He fiddled with the loose change in his pocket and avoided eye contact with me.

"Goodbye, Bryce."

"Goodbye, Traci."

We embraced one last time, and I knew it would be the last time I ever saw him. Not because he was sore about my decision not to choose him and sultry adventure. Not because we disliked each other. But because the exchange was over.

People speak of soul mates, soul families, and angels. Bryce was one of my teachers; an angel wearing a writer man outfit. Our exchange—his testing of my boundaries, of my strength to heed inner wisdom—was now over. It was over because we already had the traveler-writer romance. It was two years ago, on a beach in Nicaragua, with cheap red wine.

The Four-Point U-Turn
10.6.14

I am in New York. In my pink childhood bedroom again; the pink wallpaper I despised as a child now glows comfortingly in the lamp light. I am safe. I am with people who love me. And I am ready to face whatever demons are attached to me.

The journey home to my parents' homestead had four parts. Four, excruciating, potential-for-panic parts. I met the taxi driver outside of Karen's house at 5 a.m. The stars were out, and it was cold enough to see my breath. I dove in and knew there were only two ways this was going down: either I would have a panic attack again on some form of transit on the way to NY, and address it at that time, or not, and make it to New York with just a very elevated heart rate.

I flopped into the taxi and surrendered to the options that lay ahead.

The taxi ride was short and uneventful. Because it was so early, and so unseasonably cold, the driver insisted on dropping me off not at the bus stop but at the swanky hotel the airport shuttle began its route at.

I stood inside for fifteen minutes in the lobby, breathing deeply and pacing nervously. I still hadn't completely surrendered. Actually I had not surrendered at all. I was still trying to stave it off like a tribute in *The Hunger Games* staves off their opponent. Surrender is so difficult, especially after the week I had.

The airport shuttle pulled up, me and ten other older folks ambled into the van and departed the historic downtown. I was leaving Santa Fe. The road trip is over. Now what?

The idea of now what puzzled and nauseated me, so I grabbed for my tiny off-brand MP3 player and put one of my favorite India Arie songs on loop. I closed my eyes, held the Arkansas crystal Scott had given me with an iron grip, and the shuttle made its two-thousand-foot descent to the Albuquerque airport. This was the hardest part. This was the stretch of the I-25 where I froze up a week ago and life smacked me upside the head. This was it. A few times I could feel the energy of anxiety surge. I breathed in the music.

You got this. No panic. I know. This hurts. This is where life halted on the northbound side. Yes, dear one, it will all be ok soon. Yes, it is okay to feel very sad. Inhale Traci, inhale deeply. I tried to comfort myself. That, combined with my prairie man's crystal, seemed to quell me.

Sixty miles later I was past the scene of the crime. Two parts of the unexpected U-turn were over. Two flights—one to Midway and the second to Albany—stood in front of me, my tethered heart still beating rapid fire.

The thunder of panic rose here and there on the first flight. I've flown a million times, and this flight happened to be very turbulent. In an effort to stay focused, I read the Skymall magazine three times; it's safe to say the lady next to be thought I was obsessed with dogs in absurd rain protective gear. I drank ginger ale like a champ but couldn't really find comfort in the pretzel giveaways.

I was the last shmuck off the first flight, barely making my connection to the plane bound for Albany. Thankfully the gates were only two away, because I am not sure I would have even attempted to run. Every leg of the U-turn wore me down. I was shutting down. Conserving every last ounce of clear-headed human energy I had.

You got this, Traci. Final leg. Step four of four. In three hours you will be home in your pink bedroom with Mom and Dad.

The final flight wasn't the least bit epic. A part of me wishes I could tell you something incredibly thrilling or odd happened. Like that prairie man Scott happened to be on the same plane and we joined the mile-high club, my rapid heart rate suddenly not a problem for high-altitude sex. Or that the lady next to me owned a tiny home in Ithaca and would help me build one.

Nope. Not a bloody thing of note the whole flight. My heart still raced, I went in and out of light sleep, never thankfully having another full blown anxiety moment.

"Please put away your electronic devices, buckle your seatbelts, and return your chair to its upright position, as we make our final descent into Albany," the captain's chipper voice woke me.

"Is Albany home for you?" The large lady next to me asked.

"Yes. Er, yes. It is. I am going home. I am going home," I said it twice, actually absorbing the truth of things.

Can you feel the beginning and end of things? How does life indicate the page has been turned?

That moment, when the airplane wheels hit the tarmac with gruff force, my brain slammed to my knees. Tears erupted from my eyeballs and I closed them, trying to contain it. But I had no power of restraint left. I began to weep. An old part of my life just ended, and a new part has just taken its first look at the new horizon. There was still shrapnel of my broken heart in all the places I had traveled, but unexpectedly I had a new thought.

That maybe, just maybe, I didn't need those old pieces. There was no point to recovering them, because, unless you build salvaged tiny homes in Luling, Texas, you don't need old parts for new things. I continued to weep and both of my seatmates had no idea what was going on. They didn't know that my car was being escorted to Florida. They didn't know about the active volcano in my stomach. They just looked awkwardly at each other and murmured, "She must have been gone a long time."

My inner self, the little lady who likes to emerge with a big stick from my belly button, came out to witness me weep. She watched for a moment, I cleared my throat.

"Now the real work begins," she said, and smiled confidently at me.

I walk-cried all the way to baggage claim and let it fall out of me. I didn't care who watched. Luckily my brown suitcase was one of the first suitcases to roll around the carousel. I grabbed it quickly, shouldered my backpack, and went outside to look for my mom's red truck.

I saw her coming up the sidewalk, the truck parked in a no-parking zone down the way. This was one of those epic moments. Like Hallmark-movie *epic.*

I let her run at me; I wasn't about to run, and dropped all of my bags to the ground. I stood there, metaphorically hoisting the white flag, and howled loudly. I was an incredibly hot fucking mess of twenty-eight years of living full out.

"Traci Ann, I love you," said the woman who gave birth to me. She wrapped her arms around me and nothing mattered anymore. I let her hold me. She let me hold on. The level of love I felt, and release that came with it was nothing short of otherworldly.

Something ended today. Something new started. And there was work to be done.

About Traci Ann

Traci Ann is inside of this book. All of her dirty little secrets and sassy stories. Yours are, too. All you have to do is say yes—pack all of your shit, put on your big girl pants and follow your heart, in whatever direction it pulls.

Warning: Traci has been known to inspire over coffee, beer and dehydrated rice and beans. Upon meeting Traci, you may quit your job, sell your house and travel into your depths.

TRACI ANN